FEDERICO GARCÍA LORCA

SELECTED POEMS

Merryn Williams is an Anglo-Welsh poet who works as a full-time writer and part-time tutor. Born in Devon in 1944, the daughter of the writer Raymond Williams, she grew up on the South Coast, and was educated mainly at grammar school in Hastings. After studying English at New Hall and Darwin College, Cambridge, she obtained a Ph.D. on the novels of Thomas Hardy and then worked for a year at the Open University, for which she still does part-time teaching. She is married to a physicist at Cranfield Institute and lives with her family in Wootton, Bedfordshire.

Her works include *Preface to Hardy* (1982), *Women in the English Novel 1800–1900* (1984), *Margaret Oliphant: A Critical Biography* (1986) and *Six Women Novelists* (1987), all published by Macmillan. She has a special interest in the Scottish Victorian novelist Margaret Oliphant and has been instrumental in getting some of her neglected books back into print. In 1985 she began to publish poetry and has appeared with four other Anglo-Welsh poets in the Seren Books anthology *The Bloodstream* (1989). She has been interested in Lorca and the Spanish Civil War for many years.

Some of these translations have appeared in *Acumen, Ambit, The Frogmore Papers, The Honest Ulsterman, Outposts, Oxford Poetry, Poetry Durham, The Rialto* and *Spokes*. These translations are dedicated to the Open University poets.

FEDERICO GARCÍA LORCA

SELECTED POEMS

TRANSLATED BY
MERRYN WILLIAMS

BLOODAXE BOOKS

Spanish texts from *Obras Completas*, volume I (Aguilar, 1987 edition) and *Conferencias*, volume II (Alianza Editorial, 1984), copyright © 1992 by Herederos de Federico García Lorca. English translations of Spanish texts of *Sonetas del amor oscuro / Sonnets of Dark Love* copyright © 1992 by Herederos de Federico García Lorca and Merryn Williams. English translations of other Spanish texts copyright © Merryn Williams 1992.

ISBN: 1 85224 160 8

First published 1992 by
Bloodaxe Books Ltd,
P.O. Box 1SN,
Newcastle upon Tyne NE99 1SN.

Bloodaxe Books Ltd acknowledges
the financial assistance of Northern Arts.

Cover reproduction by V & H Reprographics, Newcastle upon Tyne.

Cover printing by Index Print, Newcastle upon Tyne.

Printed in Great Britain by
Bell & Bain Limited, Glasgow, Scotland.

CONTENTS

INTRODUCTION

In the half-century since Lorca's murder his plays have been performed throughout Europe and America with great success. His poetry, apart from 'Lament for Ignacio Sánchez Mejías' and some of the gypsy ballads, is less well-known in this country. Yet all over the Spanish-speaking world he is recognised as one of the very greatest modern poets. It is hoped that these translations will give him a higher profile among English readers, especially now that his *Sonnets of Dark Love*, lost for nearly fifty years, have been found.

Federico García Lorca was born on 5th June 1898, a few months after another great poet-dramatist, Brecht. His father, Federico García Rodríguez, was a landowner in Fuente Vaqueros, Andalucía; his mother, Vicenta Lorca Romero, had been a schoolmistress. The family had grown moderately rich through the sugar beet boom, but their relations had been landless labourers. There were four younger children, one of whom, Luis, died in infancy. This may be why the image of the dead child reverberates through Lorca's work.

The poet remembered his early years as a magic time. He grew up in what was then one of the most beautiful parts of Europe, and in a small friendly community scarcely touched by industrialism:

> I love the countryside. I feel myself linked to it in all my emotions. My oldest childhood memories have the flavour of the earth...Were this not so I could not have written *Blood Wedding*.

According to his brother Francisco, the people really did talk as they do in the plays: 'One time Dolores was describing the birth of a spring and in her picturesque and vivid speech she said "...and imagine, a bull of water rose up".'(Lorca would use the bull/water image in his 'Ballad of the Doomed Man'). Illiterate nurses and servants transmitted a rich oral culture to the middle-class children they cared for. Lorca as an adult remained fascinated by the ancient lullabies and ballads of Andalucía. Ultimately their message was a harsh one, 'alone you are, alone you always will be'.

The history of southern Spain was intensely real to the child. When he was eight, he saw a Roman mosaic uncovered in the fields; when he was eleven, the family moved to Granada, a city full of fountains, exotic flowers, views of the Sierra and marvellous Arab architecture. The people of his region included many gypsies and descendants of Moors and Jews who had been forcibly converted to Catholicism in the fifteenth century. Lorca believed that his own blood was mixed and identified with the ethnic minorities, as we now call them:

> Coming from Granada gives me a fellow feeling for those who are persecuted. For the gypsy, the negro, the Jew, the Moor, whom all *granadinos* carry inside them.

The city was beautiful, but dominated by a middle class which was bigoted and philistine. Lorca felt afterwards that the move to Granada marked the end of his childhood (as hinted in the poem '1910'). The boys at his new school called him 'Federica' and despised him for his clumsiness (one leg was shorter than the other, which got him out of doing military service). It seems he was a gifted musician and wanted to study in Paris, but his father insisted he should train for a conventional career. Like the boy in 'Suicide', he probably went through agonies because he could not do his geometry. But in his late teens he began to write poems and read them to the groups of lively young people who hung about the cafés of Granada. Young as he was he was a born performer and made an extraordinary impression.

In 1919 he moved to Madrid, officially to study law (in which he finally managed with great difficulty to get a degree). He lodged at the Residencia de Estudiantes, a famous institution run on liberal non-sectarian lines. Here he met other brilliant young Spaniards, including Luis Buñuel the future film director, and wrote an avant-garde play, *The Butterfly's Evil Spell*, which was booed off the stage. Without being involved in politics, he and his friends believed that deep changes were needed in Spain. The country was much more backward than the rest of Europe; the contrast between rich and poor was glaring; the Catholic church had unacceptable privileges and the cultural establishment seemed to them hopelessly behind the times.

His sympathy for the avant-garde was strengthened by his friendship with Salvador Dalí, whom he met in 1923. Lorca was excited by his 'huge, extraordinarily expressive squares of burning paint' and also obsessed by him as a man. By this time he had realised he was homosexual, a fact he could not reveal to his parents and which caused him deep unhappiness. He undoubtedly loved Dalí (to whom he wrote a well-known Ode), but it seems there was no physical relationship.

Yet, for all his 'modernism' (he liked to claim he had been born in 1900, to stamp himself as a man of the new century), he was still deeply rooted in the traditional culture of Spain. He was a friend of the composer Manuel de Falla, with whom he organised a flamenco festival in 1922. His early poems were very simple lyrics which went straight to the hearts of ordinary people. He preferred to read them aloud rather than print them, so his reputation was high among fellow-writers at a time when he had published very little. Meanwhile he resisted getting a job, assuring his father that he would soon make a breakthrough as a playwright.

The first breakthrough came when his play, *Mariana Pineda*, was staged in 1927. The following year he published *Gypsy Ballads* which had a vast and immediate success. He still did not, though, possess a settled income and remained humiliatingly dependent on his parents.

Accounts of him give the impression of a great charmer, multi-talented (he could draw and sing as well as write and play), impractical in daily life and a natural victim. One is from an old peasant woman:

> He wasn't brave...He was a very kind person. When he was around nobody went hungry.

Another, from an English acquaintance:

> On the surface he seemed lively, even gay, but what struck me most was the sad look in his eyes, the kind of sadness that one sees in the eyes of an animal, not because they are hurt or suffering from anything in particular but a kind of elemental sorrow for the nature of things.

That dates from 1929 when Lorca was passing through England (his only visit) en route for New York. He was then suffering from a serious depression and wanted a complete break with the Old World. But the United States, where Wall Street was about to crash, did not make him feel any better; he went into culture-shock and spent the next nine months writing the extraordinary poems which were collected, after his death, in *Poet in New York*. It left him with a hatred of industrial capitalism and an abiding sympathy for the American blacks. He was glad to head for Cuba, where his *Gypsy Ballads* were already famous, and then to go home.

Next year, 1931, Spain became a republic and Lorca, like most intellectuals, believed that they were at the start of a new and hopeful age. As well as other very necessary reforms, the new government was anxious to spread education and culture. 'Illiteracy blinds the spirit', as a Civil War poster would say. He became director of a student theatre company, La Barraca, which travelled round the villages (heavily harassed by the Right) performing the great Spanish classics to peasants who had never seen a play before, and were thrilled. Although the object was not to promote his own plays, it gave him invaluable experience. Over the next few years he spent more time on drama, less on lyric poetry.

The first of his great plays, *Blood Wedding*, was performed in 1933 and had an outstanding success in Spain and then Argentina. He was wildly popular in Buenos Aires which he visited later that year. At long last he was gaining money (which he lavishly gave away) and fame. But he was anxious not to lose touch with ordinary people:

> I will always be on the side of those who have nothing [*he said in a newspaper interview in 1934*]...We – and by we I mean those of us who are intellectuals, educated in well-off middle-class families – are being called to make sacrifices. Let's accept the challenge.

By now the rising Fascist movement knew him for an enemy and when his play *Yerma* was staged they abused it from the audience and in print. His fame continued to grow in Spain and Latin America and he continued to show his solidarity with what the young and vulnerable Republic was trying to do. A manifesto signed by him and other intellectuals early in 1936 stated that 'we want liberty to be respected, the standard of living raised and culture brought to the widest possible range of Spaniards'.

The Civil War which broke out in July, just after Lorca had finished his last play *The House of Bernarda Alba*, found him in Granada, one of the first towns to fall to Franco. In the white terror that followed, about five thousand people in this region were murdered.

Exactly what happened to Lorca was a mystery for many years but was reconstructed in great detail in the 1970s by Ian Gibson. His sister's husband was under arrest (later to be shot), and he realised that he too was in danger when a group of men turned up at his parents' home, beat up the caretaker, and told Lorca that they knew all about him and were going to get him. It was decided that he should stay with a fellow poet, Luis Rosales, whose family were Fascists. But on 16th August someone denounced him and he was taken away by a police escort, one of whom said that he was a Russian spy and 'had done more damage with his pen than others with their guns'. He remained in custody for two or three nights; apparently the Civil Governor was unsure about whether to kill him but got official permission to go ahead. In the small hours of 18th or 19th August, a young friend, Ricardo Rodríguez Jímenez happened to see him being brought out of the police station. Jímenez had been partially paralysed as a child, and Lorca had characteristically got him a small violin so that he could learn to play:

> His right hand was handcuffed to that of a schoolmaster from La Zubia with white hair...Someone stuck a gun in my chest. I screamed: 'Murderers! You're going to kill a genius! A genius! Murderers!'

Lorca and the schoolmaster, with two anarchist bullfighters, were driven to the village of Viznar at the foot of the Sierra and kept there for a few hours until dawn. They were then shot and buried in a shallow trench among the olive trees, near the famous spring of Fuente Grande. Many hundreds of other victims lie there, and it is impossible to pinpoint the exact place of Lorca's grave.

'But all should know that I have not died'. It was not possible to wipe out Lorca's poetry or his reputation, and almost at once Franco's forces began to distance themselves from the murder. The news went round the world; Lorca became a symbol of the martyrdom of Spain. The Fascists put out various statements suggesting that he had been killed by someone else and that he was not political anyway, but nevertheless it was unsafe to talk about him in Franco's Spain for many years. Elsewhere, the fame of his plays and poems grew steadily. His *Complete Works* (not really complete) were eventually published with the dictator's permission in 1954. When the country became a democracy again more poems became available, as well as Ian Gibson's invaluable accounts of his life and death. He is now as famous, and as widely-loved, in Spanish-speaking countries as Shakespeare in our own.

It is easy to overpraise poets who die young or who are political martyrs, but that is not the reason for Lorca's tremendous and universal appeal. 'Everyone who reads a poem of Lorca's falls in love with him,' wrote Robert Bly, 'and has a secret friend'. Even the pro-Franco Roy Campbell fell under the spell and translated him. Yet if a poem is taken out of its own language and transplanted into a completely different culture, how much is left?

I decided to test this by printing my translation of 'The Faithless Wife' in a magazine which circulates privately among (mostly) unpublished poets. The response amazed me. Those who knew the Spanish text pointed out that a great deal had been lost, but those reading it for the first time were enthusiastic:

'Those wonderful sensual images, the interplay of emotion and landscape, and the sense of otherness...'

'I like the imagery immensely...'

'It is a powerful piece and succeeds because of the simplicity of its subject matter (it is simple in the sense that the sexual act is something we can all claim to understand) and the corresponding simplicity of the language...'

'You speak of what it has "lost in translation" but it can surely have lost none of the arresting sharpness of the imagery.'

Imagery, simplicity, emotion; these are the words to bear in mind when trying to understand Lorca's appeal. They explain, perhaps, why he is so good at leaping barriers.

It is a very different kind of poetry from that which most English readers admire. Consider one of our own poets who has been strikingly successful at communicating with ordinary people, Philip Larkin. (Or, if you like, compare and contrast his 'Church Going' with Lorca's 'Cry to Rome'). Here is a wry, understated poetry about the awfulness of going out to work or living in rented rooms, about mothers-in-law and the pies on British Rail and the men in white coats. The great themes are there in the background but it is unusual for such an "English" poet as Larkin to confront them directly. Lorca was aware of our reputation for *sang-froid* (literally translated, 'cold blood'). In his ballad 'Preciosa and the Wind', a gypsy girl fleeing from a rapist invades the British consulate and is offered a glass of warm milk, thus near-tragedy gives way to humour. Did he think that the English prefer a milk-and-water poetry?

In 1928 Lorca described his artistic creed as 'a return to inspiration, pure instinct, the poet's only reason. I cannot bear logical poetry...Passion and instinct'. He said much the same in 1935, referring to an image in 'Somnambular Ballad':

> If you ask me why I wrote 'A thousand glass tambourines/wounded the dawn', I will tell you that I saw them, in the hands of angels and trees, but I will not be able to say more; certainly I cannot explain their meaning. And that is the way it should be. By means of poetry a man more rapidly approaches the cutting edge that the philosopher and the mathematician turn away from in silence.

Yet he did not go along with the view that poetry must be difficult. 'He addressed himself to simple persons,' wrote his brother Francisco, 'or to what there can be of simplicity in persons who are not simple.' If we look at the themes of his three great plays, we find that all are of a blinding simplicity. A wedding which ends in blood; a wife who eats her heart out because she is childless and eventually murders her husband; a houseful of girls shut away from the light and men, one of whom breaks the rules and then hangs herself. These are the kind of stories you might read in the tabloid press and they remind us forcibly of the cliché that poetry is about only two things, love and death.

'The Faithless Wife' has a near-universal appeal, as has been said, because it is about sex (not love). 'Thamar and Amnón' describes the agonies of frustration culminating in rape. The *Sonnets of Dark Love* and several of the *Diván del Tamarit* poems deal with the kind of love we find in Housman's *Shropshire Lad* – love that is 'dark', one-sided, frustrated or at any rate unlikely to end happily. Here again Lorca is tapping into a universal theme.

Death is on the margin of all these poems, if only because the writer is tormented and yearns for an end to suffering ('Gacela of the Dark Death'). All poets are obsessed by death, it is said, but Lorca was super-obsessed. The smallest things frightened him; he played games which involved pretending to be a corpse; he wrote some extraordinary lines which appear to forecast what eventually happened to him:

> ...comprendí que me habían asesinado.
> Recorrieron los cafés y los cementerios y las iglesias,
> abrieron los toneles y los armarios,
> destrozaron tres esqueletos para arrancar sus dientes de oro.
> Ya no me encontraron.
> ¿No me encontraron?
> No. No me encontraron.
>
> ['Fábula y rueda de los tres amigos']

which translates:

> I realised I had been murdered.
> They searched cafés, cemeteries, churches.
> They opened barrels and cupboards.
> And plundered three skeletons for their gold teeth.
> But they never found me.
> They never found me?
> No. They never found me.
>
> ['Fable and Round of the Three Friends']

This death-fixation may be traced back to his early years when he had been brought up on gory tales about Catholic martyrs, allowed to view corpses and probably seen the bone-pits of Andalucía where dead animals were dumped ('the horse's motionless skull' in 'Gacela of the Flight'). He would also have been aware of the violence used against the poor and of what was happening to young men of his age just across the border in 1914-18. Certainly the Civil War would show that there was an immense potential for violence in Spain. Whatever the roots of his obsession, it made him intensely aware of the fragility of life and happiness. It also explains his fascination with the man who deliberately goes out to dice with death, like the bullfighter in his famous 'Lament for Ignacio Sánchez Mejías'. We may think this is typically Spanish, or just morbid, but it is not really very different from our own cult of the soldier. Lorca was terrified of dying and he admired bullfighters for just that reason.

This awareness of death colours almost all his work. It is what makes the early lyric, 'Song of the Rider', so powerful, but we should not expect to be told *why* the rider is doomed. If we compare it with Alfred Noyes' 'The Highwayman', which uses many of the same images, we see that it provides no background, tells no story.

Lorca shows the horse, the moon, the rider, a skeletal figure on the battlements, and that is all. Tacking a plot on to this poem would have seemed to him as old-fashioned as the story-paintings of the nineteenth century from which modern artists were trying to break free. It was enough for him to give us the basic situation, knowing we would sense that the rider is Everyman.

In the same way, the more mysterious of the gypsy poems hint at a story without telling one. In 'Ballad of the Doomed Man' Amargo (whose name means bitter) is cut off from his fellows, doomed not for any specific reason but because he is doomed. It has been pointed out that in some cultures a man will die on a given date if he is told he is going to die, but the poem cannot be bound by this narrow interpretation. Why he is singled out we don't know, but like everyone else he is moving inexorably towards death and there is nothing he can do but come to terms with it.

In 'Ballad of the Black Sorrow' Soledad (whose name means solitude) 'embodies incurable pain, the black pain we cannot get rid of except by taking a knife and opening a deep buttonhole in the left side'. The last words are Lorca's and he went on to say: 'It is a longing without object, a keen love for nothing, with the certainty that death (the eternal care of Andalucía) is breathing behind the door.'

This warns us that, again, we shouldn't try to interpret Soledad narrowly as a woman who is depressed because she has no man. She *is* sorrow (*pena*, a word repeated eight times in this poem), the 'pain of the hidden water-course and the far-distant dawn' which lies at the heart of things.

Amargo and Soledad, then, are archetypal figures, reminding us of the great unalterable facts of death and grief. Lorca's concentration on these facts, and on other basic emotions like love and aggression, goes a long way towards explaining his popularity. We do not need to have been born in his culture to understand what he is talking about; our own 'passion and instinct' make that clear.

But subject-matter in itself does not make a great poet. Lorca's genius is in the way he uses language, and as English readers we miss some of his special effects. The *Gypsy Ballads* and the sonnets, for instance, are written in extremely tight verse-forms which are almost untranslatable. What does cross the language barrier is his beautiful and sometimes startling imagery.

Certain images come up over and over again. The moon, blood, knives, bulls, horses, fish, water, sand, apples, olives, oranges, wheat, mountains, snow, *nardos* (meaning spikenard or tuberose). Some of these images, like the last, are typically Spanish. When we read about bulls, olive groves, and people who play guitars and brawl with knives it all sounds very picturesque and "foreign". Lorca's world seems excitingly different from our own and that is part of the attraction.

But consider some other images, moon, blood, water. These are all familiar from our earliest childhood and have several layers of meaning. The moon is beautiful, but also remote and sterile. In Lorca it is commonly associated with sadness and death. Blood is essential to life and also means deadly violence. Water is especially significant for Lorca, given that he came from a city which he described as 'longing for the sea'. Granada is crossed by two rivers, the Genil and Darro (which flows underground), and is full of fountains, wells and little streams. Water includes tears. It can become stagnant and can kill by drowning (as in 'Nocturnes of the Window' and 'Gacela of the Dead Child'); we know that Lorca was haunted by the memory of a little girl who had been drowned in a well. Water is also life-giving. In 'Ballad of the Black Sorrow' the central figure is told:

'Soledad, wash your body
in water of skylarks'

which suggests that there is a world outside her misery. Water is craved by the corpses in 'Gacela of the Dark Death'. In the beautiful and mysterious 'Casida of one Wounded by the Water', the poet says repeatedly 'I want to go down to the well', and associates the many 'ponds, cisterns and fountains' of Granada with the boy who is dying of wounds. Obviously it is an unnatural death, perhaps suicide, perhaps the result of a knife-fight, perhaps recalling the massacre of a generation in the Great War. There is a strong feeling that the boy needs to get close to the source of life, water, and that if anything can cure his agony that will.

Like other writers born in the nineteenth century (Thomas Hardy springs to mind) Lorca was both intensely traditional and extremely modern. On the one side he was influenced by Andalucían myths and ballads, on the other by Buster Keaton and Salvador Dalí. He created some images, like blue horses and bleeding violins, which could have come straight out of a surrealist painting. From the cinema he learned that it is possible to move very fast from one subject to another and that the image is all-important. He read Eliot in translation and was impressed.

His most sustained attempt to write as a modernist was in the New York poems, and they are so modern that some of us may find them impenetrable. If the reader has difficulty with certain passages, it is best not to worry about the exact meaning and to concentrate on the images and their emotional power. For instance, when Lorca uses the expression 'crushed reds' in 'The King of Harlem' he is referring to black people's great warmth and vitality and the fact that they are being oppressed. When he writes about moss and nettles in Wall Street ('Dance of Death'), he is protesting that modern, money-mad New York excludes natural life and forecasting that one day it will take its revenge. With the great cities of the Western world falling apart and the green movement striking a deep response, who shall say he was wrong? He did not pretend to analyse twentieth-century civilisation, but he knew in his bones, like Eliot, that it was a wasteland.

It may seem perverse that Lorca should have turned away from New York's great symbolic achievements – the skyscrapers, the millionaires – to concentrate on those parts of the city's life which seem marginal. He writes about blacks doing menial jobs, drunks, men maddened by the memory of the war and – a subject most of us prefer to forget – the huge numbers of animals which are slaughtered every day so the city can eat:

> I denounce all those
> who ignore the other half,
> the irredeemable half
> who raise their mountains of cement
> where beat the hearts
> of little animals who are forgotten
> and where we shall all go down
> in the last jamboree of drills.
>
> ['New York: Office and Denunciation']

Here Lorca is saying two things; that a civilisation founded on cruelty does not deserve to last and that his sympathies are with 'the other half', the victims.

It will be seen that my view of the poet is diametrically opposed to that of Carl W. Cobb, who thought that 'the development of the self and the creation of art were his *only* imperatives'. If Lorca had been that kind of writer, he would probably not have been killed. He became a target because he had clearly identified with ordinary people's hopes of living a better life. And although much (not all) of his work is non-political, it miraculously bridges the gap between high and popular art.

I come back to his contemporary, Brecht. On the surface, no two writers could seem more different – one a Marxist, deeply influenced by Luther's Bible, the other an anti-clerical Catholic; the

German wary of emotion and forever urging his readers to *think*, the Spaniard dominated by 'passion and instinct'. Yet both of them rejected a system which starved and thwarted people, and both wanted to write for a mass audience rather than an elite. They were both high on the Fascists' hit-list for this reason.

We have moved on, and if our own times seem terrible, it is in a different way from Lorca's Spain. Yet as we read this profoundly un-English poet, we find that, like all great writers, he is talking about problems we understand. In these translations, I have stuck fairly closely to Lorca's meaning, while trying to produce poems which are acceptable in their own right.

MERRYN WILLIAMS

SELECTED BIBLIOGRAPHY

Arturo Barea: *Lorca: The Poet and his People* (New York, 1949).
Paul Binding: *Lorca: The Gay Imagination* (London, 1985).
Ian Gibson: *The Assassination of Federico García Lorca* (London, 1979.
Ian Gibson: *Federico García Lorca: A Life* (London, 1989).
Richard L. Predmore: *Lorca's New York Poetry* (Durham, NC, 1980).

EARLY POEMS

1919-1925

EARLY POEMS

These poems, written in the 1920s, are selected from a very large body of early work. Most are short and simple, but contain images and themes which would haunt the poet all his life.

Death is a pervasive presence. It stalks in and out of the tavern, it waits before Córdoba for the lone rider (the horse is always a potent symbol in Lorca), it pushes the schoolboy in 'Suicide' towards pointless self-destruction. Even the apparently peaceful settings of 'Landscape' and 'Village' have sinister undertones, and even the guitar is weeping 'for things far away'

The moon is an absolutely central symbol. On the whole it is not a happy one; the lovely poem 'The Moon Comes Out' conjures up images of icy fruit and silver coins which weep. 'Arc of Moons', written in 1923, is an attempt by the poet to come to terms with his sexual nature, running away from the role of husband and father. (In another poem from the same cycle he sees his dead grandparents offering him a wedding ring which he rejects in horror). 'My cries turn into roses', he concludes – the Spanish word is *nardos* or spikenards – and perhaps this is a way of saying that he will use his suffering to create poetry. 'Song of the Barren Orange Tree' may also be inspired by his voluntary sterility.

Finally, there is the 'Ode to Salvador Dalí'. It was published in 1926, while Lorca was still working on the book of gypsy ballads which did not come out until two years later, and it points clearly towards the surrealist poetry he would write in New York. It is a generous tribute to a friend but also a manifesto for modern art – to quote Ian Gibson:

> Lorca admired in Dalí's work – as in that of his cubist predecessors – its symmetry, objectivity and lack of sentimentality, its flight from both outmoded realism and the 'Impressionist mist'.

Itself difficult to interpret, the Ode sings the praises of a painter who has scrapped the old rules. We are assaulted by metaphors, some of which make little sense. Modern art is cold – 'a marble iceberg' – aseptic, hygienic, obsessed with forms and limits, preferring caged birds and fish to free ones. It is also light-hearted and anti-realist; a rose is just as good as a compass at sea. 'The most heterogeneous ideas are yoked by violence together' (as Johnson wrote of the Metaphysicals), such as the bicycle of shells and coral which Dalí rides. Cadaqués is the Catalan fishing village where Lorca stayed with the painter's family, and the sea – accompanied by mermaids, sailors, ships and of course the moon – moves in and out of this poem. It is rather long, but had to be included, not only because it concerns a relationship which mattered to Lorca but also because it shows that by his late twenties he saw himself as a highly 'modern' artist.

Sueño

Mi corazón reposa junto a la fuente fría.

(Llénala con tus hilos,
araña del olvido.)

El agua de la fuente su canción le decía.

(Llénala con tus hilos,
araña del olvido.)

Mi corazón despierto sus amores decía.

(Araña del silencio,
téjele tu misterio.)

El agua de la fuente lo escuchaba sombría.

(Araña del silencio,
téjele tu misterio.)

Mi corazón se vuelca sobre la fuente fría.

(Manos blancas, lejanas,
detened a las aguas.)

Y el agua se lo lleva cantando de alegría.

(¡Manos blancas, lejanas,
nada queda en las aguas!)

[Mayo 1919]

Dream

My heart rests beside the cold fountain.

> (Fill it with your threads,
> spider of oblivion.)

The water of the fountain sang its song.

> (Fill it with your threads,
> spider of oblivion.)

My awakened heart sang of love.

> (Spider of silence,
> weave your mystery.)

The water of the fountain listened darkly.

> (Spider of silence,
> weave your mystery.)

My heart tumbles into the cold fountain.

> (White hands, far away,
> stem the waters.)

The water bears it off, joyously singing.

> (White hands, far away,
> there is nothing!)

[May 1919]

Baladilla de los tres ríos

El río Guadalquivir
va entre naranjos y olivos.
Los dos ríos de Granada
bajan de la nieve al trigo.

¡Ay, amor
que se fue y no vino!

El río Guadalquivir
tiene las barbas granates.
Los dos ríos de Granada,
uno llanto y otro sangre.

¡Ay, amor
que se fue por el aire!

Para los barcos de vela
Sevilla tiene un camino;
por el agua de Granada
solo reman los suspiros.

¡Ay, amor
que se fue y no vino!

Guadalquivir, alta torre
y viento en los naranjales.
Dauro y Genil, torrecillas
muertas sobre los estanques.

¡Ay, amor
que se fue por el aire!

¡Quién dirá que el agua lleva
un fuego fatuo de gritos!

¡Ay, amor
que se fue y no vino!

Little Ballad of Three Rivers

The river Guadalquivir flows
through orange trees and olives.
Granada's two rivers fall
from the snow to the wheat.

Ah, love that fled
and never returned!

The river Guadalquivir has
a crimson-coloured beard.
Two rivers of Granada,
one weeping and one blood.

Ah, love that fled
through the air!

For the sailing ships
Sevilla has a path;
through the waters of Granada
nothing rows but sighs.

Ah, love, that fled
and never returned!

Guadalquivir, high tower,
and wind in orange groves.
Dauro, Genil, little towers
dead above the ponds.

Ah, love, that fled
through the air!

Who will say that water bears
a will-o'-the-wisp of cries!

Ah, love, that fled
and never returned!

Lleva azahar, lleva olivas,
Andalucía, a tus mares.

¡Ay, amor
que se fue por el aire!

[Diciembre 1922]

Paisaje

El campo
de olivos
se abre y se cierra
como un abanico.
Sobre el olivar
hay un cielo hundido
y una lluvia oscura
de luceros fríos.
Tiembla junco y penumbra
a la orilla del río.
Se riza el aire gris.
Los olivos
están cargados
de gritos.
Una bandada
de pájaros cautivos,
que mueven sus larguísimas
colas en lo sombrío.

Bear orange blossom, Andalucía,
and olives to your seas.

Ah, love, that fled
through the air!

[December 1922]

Landscape

The field
of olive trees
opens and shuts
like a fan.
Above the olive grove
sunk sky
dark rain
of cold stars.
The reeds and darkness tremble
along the river bank.
The grey air ripples.
The olives
are charged
with screams.
A flock
of captive birds
which move their great
tails in shade.

La guitarra

Empieza el llanto
de la guitarra.
Se rompen las copas
de la madrugada.
Empieza el llanto
de la guitarra.
Es inútil
callarla.
Es imposible
callarla.
Llora monótona
como llora el agua,
como llora el viento
sobre la nevada.
Es imposible
callarla.
Llora por cosas
lejanas.
Arena del Sur caliente
que pide camelias blancas.
Llora flecha sin blanco,
la tarde sin mañana,
y el primer pájaro muerto
sobre la rama.
¡Oh guitarra!
Corazón malherido
por cinco espadas.

The Guitar

The wail of the guitar
begins.
The goblets of dawn
are broken.
The wail of the guitar
begins.
It is useless to hush it.
Impossible
to hush it.
It weeps, monotonous
as water weeps, as wind
weeps above the snowfall.
Impossible
to hush it.
It weeps for things
far away.
Sand of the warm South
pleading for white camelias.
It weeps, like an arrow
without a target,
an evening without dawn,
the first dead bird
on the branch.
Oh, guitar!
Heart mangled
by five swords.

Pueblo

Sobre el monte pelado
un calvario.
Agua clara
y olivos centenarios.
Por las callejas
hombres embozados,
y en las torres
veletas girando.
Eternamente
girando.
¡Oh pueblo perdido,
en la Andalucía del llanto!

Saeta

Cristo moreno
pasa
de lirio de Judea
a clavel de España.

   ¡Miradlo por dónde viene!

   De España.
Cielo limpio y oscuro,
tierra tostada,
y cauces donde corre
muy lenta el agua.
Cristo moreno,
con las guedejas quemadas,
los pómulos salientes
y las pupilas blancas.

   ¡Miradlo por dónde va!

Village

On the bare mountain stands
a Calvary.
Clear water, hundred-year-old
olive tree.
Through the narrow streets
go cloaked men.
And on the towers
weathercocks
rotating.
Yes, eternally
rotating.
Oh, lost village,
Andalucía,
in mourning!

Saeta

The dark Christ
passes from
the lily of Judea
to Spain's carnation.

Look, he is coming!

Spain's
sky clear and dark,
scorched earth,
river-beds where
very slowly runs the water.
The dark Christ,
with burned hair,
jutting cheekbones
and white pupils.

Look, he is going!

B

Camino

Cien jinetes enlutados,
¿dónde irán,
por el cielo yacente
del naranjal?
Ni a Córdoba ni a Sevilla
llegarán.
Ni a Granada la que suspira
por el mar.
Esos caballos soñolientos
los llevarán,
al laberinto de las cruces
donde tiembla el cantar.
Con siete ayes clavados,
¿dónde irán
los cien jinetes andaluces
del naranjal?

Malagueña

La muerte
entra y sale
de la taberna.

   Pasan caballos negros
y gente siniestra
por los hondos caminos
de la guitarra.

   Y hay un olor a sal
y a sangre de hembra,
en los nardos febriles
de la marina.

   La muerte
entra y sale,
y sale y entra
la muerte
de la taberna.

Journey

One hundred horsemen in mourning,
where are they going,
along the low-lying sky
of the orange grove?
Not to Córdoba or Sevilla,
nor yet to Granada,
she who sighs for the sea.
Those drowsy horses will take them
to a labyrinth of crosses
in which the song is trembling.
With seven nailed-on sorrows,
where are they going,
one hundred Andalucían horsemen
of the orange grove?

Malagueña

Death
goes in and out
of the tavern.

Black horses
and sinister people
move along the deep paths
of the guitar.

And there is a smell of salt
and a smell of woman's blood
in the feverish roses
of the sea shore.

Death
goes in and out,
and out and in
goes death
of the tavern.

Nocturnos de la ventana (4)
(A la memoria de José Ciria y Escalante, poeta)

Al estanque se le ha muerto
hoy una niña de agua.
Está fuera del estanque,
sobre el suelo amortajada.

De la cabeza a sus muslos
un pez la cruza, llamándola.
El viento le dice «niña»,
mas no puede despertarla.

El estanque tiene suelta
su cabellera de algas
y al aire sus grises tetas
estremecidas de ranas.

«Dios te salve» rezaremos
a Nuestra Señora de Agua
por la niña del estanque
muerta bajo las manzanas.

Yo luego pondré a su lado
dos pequeñas calabazas
para que se tenga a flote,
¡ay!, sobre la mar salada.

[Mayo 1923]

Arco de lunas

Un arco de lunas negras
sobre el mar sin movimiento.

Mis hijos que no han nacido
me persiguen.

Nocturnes of the Window (4)

(in memory of the poet José Ciria y Escalante)

Today, in the reservoir,
a child has died in the water.
Now she is out of the pool,
laid on the earth and shrouded.

From her head to her thighs
a fish crosses her, calls her.
The wind says, 'Child',
but they cannot wake her.

The reservoir has loosened
its hair of seaweed;
in the air its grey breasts
are shaken by frogs.

God save you. We'll pray
to Our Lady of Water
for the child from the reservoir,
under the apples, dead.

Soon I'll lay
two little gourds beside her
that she may float,
alas! on the salt sea.

[May 1923]

Arc of Moons

An arc of black moons
above the motionless sea.

My unborn children
are chasing me.

«¡Padre, no corras; espera;
el más chico viene muerto!»

Se cuelgan de mis pupilas.
Canta el gallo.

El mar, hecho piedra, ríe
su última risa de olas.

«¡Padre, no corras!...»
                                    Mis gritos
se hacen nardos.

[Julio 1923]

Canción de jinete (1860)

En la luna negra
de los bandoleros,
cantan las espuelas.

Caballito negro.
¿Dónde llevas tu jinete muerto?

...Las duras espuelas
del bandido inmóvil
que perdió las riendas.

Caballito frío.
¡Qué perfume de flor de cuchillo!

En la luna negra
sangraba el costado
de Sierra Morena.

Caballito negro.
¿Dónde llevas tu jinete muerto?

'Father, stop running, wait,
the youngest one is dead!'

They hang upon my pupils.
Crowing of a cock.

The sea, become stone,
laughs its last laugh of waves.

'Father, do not run!'...
                                My cries
turn into roses.

[July 1923]

Song of the Rider (1860)

In the black moon
of the highwaymen,
the spurs sing.

Little black horse,
where are you taking your dead rider?

...The hard spurs
of the motionless bandit,
his reins lost.

Little cold horse,
what a scent of knife-flowers!

In the black moon
bled the side
of Sierra Morena.

Little black horse,
where are you taking your dead rider?

La noche espolea
sus negros ijares
clavándose estrellas.

Caballito frío.
¡Qué perfume de flor de cuchillo!

En la luna negra,
¡un grito! y el cuerno
largo de la hoguera.

Caballito negro.
¿Dónde llevas tu jinete muerto?

[Agosto 1927]

Canción de jinete

Córdoba.
Lejana y sola.

Jaca negra, luna grande,
y aceitunas en mi alforja.
Aunque sepa los caminos
yo nunca llegaré a Córdoba.

Por el llano, por el viento,
jaca negra, luna roja.
La muerte me está mirando
desde las torres de Córdoba.

¡Ay qué camino tan largo!
¡Ay mi jaca valerosa!
¡Ay que la muerte me espera,
antes de llegar a Córdoba!

Córdoba.
Lejana y sola.

[Julio 1924]

The night spurs
her black flanks,
nails herself with stars.

Little cold horse,
what a scent of knife-flowers!

In the black moon,
a scream!
the long horn of the bonfire.

Little black horse,
where are you taking your dead rider?

[August 1927]

Song of the Rider

Córdoba, Córdoba,
far away and solitary.

Black pony, full moon
and olives in my saddle-bag.
Although I know the roads ahead
I'll never reach Córdoba.

Through the wind, through the plain,
black pony, red moon.
Death is watching me from
the towers of Córdoba.

Ah, how long the road is!
Ah, my valiant pony!
Death is waiting for me
before I reach Córdoba.

Córdoba, Córdoba,
far away and solitary.

[July 1924]

La luna asoma

Cuando sale la luna
se pierden las campanas
y aparecen las sendas
impenetrables.

Cuando sale la luna,
el mar cubre la tierra
y el corazón se siente
isla en el infinito.

Nadie come naranjas
bajo la luna llena.
Es preciso comer
fruta verde y helada.

Cuando sale la luna
de cien rostros iguales,
la moneda de plata
solloza en el bolsillo.

Murió al amanecer

Noche de cuatro lunas
y un solo árbol,
con una sola sombra
y un solo pájaro.

Busco en mi carne las
huellas de tus labios.
El manantial besa al viento
sin tocarlo.

Llevo el No que me diste,
en la palma de la mano,
como un limón de cera
casi blanco.

The Moon Comes Out

When the moon comes out
the bells fade into silence
and impenetrable paths
come to light.

When the moon comes out
the sea floods earth's surface,
the heart feels like an island
in the infinite.

Nobody eats oranges
under the full moon.
You eat only green
and icy fruit.

When the moon comes out,
one hundred identical faces,
the silver coins in your pocket
weep.

He Died at Dawn

Night of four moons,
one solitary tree,
one solitary shadow,
one solitary bird.

I seek in my flesh
the traces of your lips.
The fountain kisses the wind
and doesn't touch it.

I carry the No that you gave me
in my palm,
like a wax lemon
almost without colour.

Noche de cuatro lunas
y un solo árbol.
En la punta de una aguja
está mi amor ¡girando!

[publicades antes en abril de 1927]

La soltera en misa

Bajo el Moisés del incienso,
adormecida.

Ojos de toro te miraban.
Tu rosario llovía.

Con ese traje de profunda seda,
no te muevas, Virginia.

Da los negros melones de tus pechos
al rumor de la misa.

Despedida

Si muero,
dejad el balcón abierto.

El niño come naranjas.
(Desde mi balcón lo veo.)

El segador siega el trigo.
(Desde mi balcón lo siento.)

¡Si muero,
dejad el balcón abierto!

[1928]

Night of four moons,
one solitary tree.
Upon the point of a pin
my love is spinning.

[first published April 1927]

The Spinster at Mass

Beneath the Moses of the incense,
drowsing.

The bull's eyes watched you.
Your rosary raining.

In that dress of deep silk,
do not move, Virginia.

Give your breasts' black melons
to the murmur of the mass.

Farewell

If I die,
leave the balcony open.

The child is eating oranges.
(From my balcony I see him.)

The harvester scythes the wheat.
(From my balcony I hear him.)

If I die,
leave the balcony open!

[1928]

Suicidio

(Quizás fue por no saberte la Geometría)

El jovencillo se olvidaba.
Eran las diez de la mañana.

Su corazón se iba llenando
de alas rotas y flores de trapo.

Notó que ya no le quedaba
en la boca más que una palabra.

Y al quitarse los guantes, caía,
de sus manos, suave ceniza.

Por el balcón se veía una torre.
El se sintió balcón y torre.

Vio, sin duda, cómo le miraba
el reloj detenido en su caja.

Vio su sombra tendida y quieta
en el blanco diván de seda.

Y el joven rígido, geométrico,
con un hacha rompió el espejo.

Al romperlo, un gran chorro de sombra
inundó la quimérica alcoba.

[23 julio 1924]

Suicide

(Perhaps it happened because you did not know your geometry)

The boy was growing faint and weak.
It was morning, ten o'clock.

His heart was filled with broken wings
and rag-flowers, feeble worthless things.

He felt that there was only one
word for his mouth to close upon.

On taking off his gloves, he saw
soft ashes falling to the floor.

Through the window, he saw a tower.
He was the window and the tower.

No doubt he also saw the clock
watch him, unmoving in its box.

He saw his quiet shadow stretched
flat out upon the white silk couch.

And, geometrical and rigid,
he broke the mirror with a hatchet.

At which, a giant jet of gloom
burst into the unreal room.

[23 July 1924]

Granada y 1850

Desde mi cuarto
oigo el surtidor.

Un dedo de la parra
y un rayo de sol
señalan hacia el sitio
de mi corazón.

Por el aire de agosto
se van las nubes. Yo,
sueño que no sueño
dentro del surtidor.

Dos marinos en la orilla

1.°
Se trajo en el corazón
un pez del Mar de la China.

A veces se ve cruzar
diminuto por sus ojos.

Olvida siendo marino
los bares y las naranjas.

Mira al agua.

2.°
Tenía la lengua de jabón.
Lavó sus palabras y se calló.

Mundo plano, mar rizado,
cien estrellas y su barco.

Vio los balcones del Papa
y los pechos dorados de las cubanas.

Mira al agua.

Granada and 1850

From my room
I hear the fountain.

A tendril of vine,
a ray of sunshine.
They point to where my heart
is beating.

Through the August air,
clouds drifting.
I dream I do not dream
within the fountain.

Two Sailors on the Beach

No.1

In his heart he wears
a fish from the China Sea.

At times you see it cruising
diminished in his eyes.

A seaman, he forgets
the bars and the oranges.

He looks at the water.

No.2

He had a tongue of soap.
He washed his words and was silent.

Flat world and curling sea,
a hundred stars and his ship.

He saw the balconies of the Pope,
the Cuban girls' golden breasts.

He looks at the water.

Canción del naranjo seco

Leñador.
Córtame la sombra.
Líbrame del suplicio
de verme sin toronjas.

    ¿Por qué nací entre espejos?
El día me da vueltas.
Y la noche me copia
en todas sus estrellas.

    Quiero vivir sin verme.
Y hormigas y vilanos,
soñaré que son mis
hojas y mis pájaros.

    Leñador.
Córtame la sombra.
Líbrame del suplicio
de verme sin toronjas.

Song of the Barren Orange Tree

Woodcutter,
cut my shadow.
Deliver me from the torture
of seeing myself fruitless.

Why was I born surrounded
by mirrors? The day turns round me.
And night reproduces me
in every one of her stars.

I want to live without seeing
myself. And I shall dream
that ants and husks have changed
into my birds and foliage.

Woodcutter,
cut my shadow.
Deliver me from the torture
of seeing myself fruitless.

Oda a Salvador Dalí

Una rosa en el alto jardín que tú deseas.
Una rueda en la pura sintaxis del acero.
Desnuda la montaña de niebla impresionista.
Los grises oteando sus balaustradas últimas.

   Los pintores modernos, en sus blancos estudios,
cortan la flor aséptica de la raíz cuadrada.
En las aguas del Sena un iceberg de mármol
enfría las ventanas y disipa las yedras.

   El hombre pisa fuerte las calles enlosadas.
Los cristales esquivan la magia del reflejo.
El Gobierno ha cerrado las tiendas de perfume.
La máquina eterniza sus compases binarios.

   Una ausencia de bosques, biombos y entrecejos
yerra por los tejados de las casas antiguas.
El aire pulimenta su prisma sobre el mar
y el horizonte sube como un gran acueducto.

   Marineros que ignoran el vino y la penumbra
decapitan sirenas en los mares de plomo.
La Noche, negra estatua de la prudencia, tiene
el espejo redondo de la luna en su mano.

   Un deseo de formas y límites nos gana.
Viene el hombre que mira con el metro amarillo.
Venus es una blanca naturaleza muerta
y los coleccionistas de mariposas huyen.

                          *

   Cadaqués, en el fiel del agua y la colina,
eleva escalinatas y oculta caracolas.
Las flautas de madera pacifican el aire.
Un viejo Dios silvestre da frutas a los niños.

   Sus pescadores duermen, sin ensueño, en la arena.
En alta mar les sirve de brújula una rosa.
El horizonte virgen de pañuelos heridos
junta los grandes vidrios del pez y de la luna.

Ode to Salvador Dalí

A rose in the high garden that you desire.
A wheel in steel's pure syntax.
Naked is the mountain of Impressionist mist.
The grey looks down upon their last balustrades.

Modern painters, in their white studios,
cut the square root's aseptic flower.
In the waters of the Seine a marble iceberg
cools the windows and dispels the ivy.

The man treads strongly on flagstoned streets.
The crystals shun the magic of reflection.
The Government has closed the scent shops.
The machine drags out its binary rhythms.

An absence of woods, folding screens and frowns
wanders over the roofs of ancient houses.
Air polishes its prism above the sea
and the horizon goes up like a great aqueduct.

Sailors who ignore the wine and the half-light
behead mermaids on seas of lead.
The Night, black statue of wisdom,
is holding the moon's round mirror.

A desire for forms and limits overcomes us.
The man who thinks with the yellow ruler is coming.
Venus is a white still-life
and the butterfly collectors flee.

*

Cadaqués, in the needle of water and the hill,
raises fire escapes and hides the shells.
Wooden flutes soothe the air.
An old Sylvan god gives fruit to the children.

Her fishermen sleep, without dreaming, on the sand.
On the high seas a rose serves them for a compass.
The horizon, free from wounded handkerchiefs,
joins great glasses of fish and the moon.

Una dura corona de blancos bergantines
ciñe frentes amargas y cabellos de arena.
Las sirenas convencen, pero no sugestionan,
y salen si mostramos un vaso de agua dulce.

*

¡Oh Salvador Dalí, de voz aceitunada!
No elogio tu imperfecto pincel adolescente
ni tu color que ronda la color de tu tiempo,
pero alabo tus ansias de eterno limitado.

Alma higiénica, vives sobre mármoles nuevos.
Huyes la oscura selva de formas increíbles.
Tu fantasía llega donde llegan tus manos,
y gozas el soneto del mar en tu ventana.

El mundo tiene sordas penumbras y desorden,
en los primeros términos que el humano frecuenta.
Pero ya las estrellas, ocultando paisajes,
señalan el esquema perfecto de sus órbitas.

La corriente del tiempo se remansa y ordena
en las formas numéricas de un siglo y otro siglo
Y la Muerte vencida se refugia temblando
en el círculo estrecho del minuto presente.

Al coger tu paleta, con un tiro en un ala,
pides la luz que anima la copa del olivo.
Ancha luz de Minerva, constructora de andamios,
donde no cabe el sueño ni su flora inexacta.

Pides la luz antigua que se queda en la frente,
sin bajar a la boca ni al corazón del hombre.
Luz que temen las vides entrañables de Baco
y la fuerza sin orden que lleva el agua curva.

Haces bien en poner banderines de aviso
en el límite oscuro que relumbra de noche.
Como pintor no quieres que te ablande la forma
el algodón cambiante de una nube imprevista.

El pez en la pecera y el pájaro en la jaula.
No quieres inventarlos en el mar o en el viento.
Estilizas o copias después de haber mirado
con honestas pupilas sus cuerpecillos ágiles.

A hard crown of white sailing-ships
encircles bitter foreheads, hair of sand.
The mermaids convince, but they do not fascinate,
and emerge if we show a vase of sweet water.

*

Oh Salvador Dalí, with the olive-coloured voice!
I don't praise your imperfect adolescent paintbrush
nor your colour which goes round the colour of your time,
but your yearning for everlasting limits.

Hygienic soul, you dwell above new marbles.
You flee the dark wood of incredible forms.
Your imagination reaches where your hands do,
you have the sonnet of the sea in your window.

The world has deaf half-lights and confusion
in the first boundaries which humans frequent.
But already the stars, concealing landscapes,
point out their orbits' perfect plan.

The flow of time grows stagnant and arranges
in numerical forms each and every century.
And defeated Death takes refuge, trembling
in the narrow circle of the present minute.

To seize your palette, with a shot in the wing,
you ask for light which animates the olives' crown.
Broad light of Minerva, constructress of scaffolds,
where the dream won't fit, or its imprecise flower.

You ask for the ancient light which burns on the forehead,
not descending to man's mouth or his heart.
Light which is feared by the dense vines of Bacchus
and the brute strength that lifts the curved water.

You do well to place little warning flags
on the dark boundary that gleams by night.
As a painter, you don't want to soften the form,
the changing cotton of an unexpected cloud.

The fish in the fishbowl and the bird in the cage.
You won't invent them in sea or in wind.
You design or you copy after having looked
clear-sighted, at their agile little bodies.

Amas una materia definida y exacta
donde el hongo no pueda poner su campamento.
Amas la arquitectura que construye en lo ausente
y admites la bandera como una simple broma.

Dice el compás de acero su corto verso elástico.
Desconocidas islas desmienten ya la esfera.
Dice la línea recta su vertical esfuerzo
y los sabios cristales cantan sus geometrías.

*

Pero también la rosa del jardín donde vives.
¡Siempre la rosa, siempre, norte y sur de nosotros!
Tranquila y concentrada como una estatua ciega,
ignorante de esfuerzos soterrados que causa.

Rosa pura que limpia de artificios y croquis
y nos abre las alas tenues de la sonrisa.
(Mariposa clavada que medita su vuelo.)
Rosa del equilibrio sin dolores buscados.
¡Siempre la rosa!

*

¡Oh Salvador Dalí, de voz aceitunada!
Digo lo que me dicen tu persona y tus cuadros.
No alabo tu imperfecto pincel adolescente,
pero canto la firme dirección de tus flechas.

Canto tu bello esfuerzo de luces catalanas,
tu amor a lo que tiene explicación posible.
Canto tu corazón astronómico y tierno,
de baraja francesa y sin ninguna herida.

Canto el ansia de estatua que persigues sin tregua,
el miedo a la emoción que te aguarda en la calle.
Canto la sirenita de la mar que te canta
montada en bicicleta de corales y conchas.

Pero ante todo canto un común pensamiento
que nos une en las horas oscuras y doradas.
No es el Arte la luz que nos ciega los ojos.
Es primero el amor, la amistad o la esgrima.

You love a definite, exact material
where the mushroom can't pitch its camp.
You love the architecture that builds in what is absent
and accept the flag as a simple joke.

You show the steel compass its short, springy verse.
Unknown islands now clash with the globe.
You show to the straight line its vertical effort
and the learned crystals sing of their geometries.

*

But also the rose of the garden you live in.
North and south of us, always the rose!
Calm and concentrated like a blind statue, not knowing
the hidden efforts it causes.

Pure rose which cleans crafts and sketches, and opens
to us the frail wings of a smile.
(Pierced butterfly thinking of flying).
Equilibrium's rose with no searching griefs.
Always the rose!

*

Oh, Salvador Dalí, with the olive-coloured voice!
I say what they say of your person and your art.
I don't praise your imperfect adolescent paintbrush,
but I sing the firm direction of your arrows.

I sing your beautiful strength of Catalan lights,
your love for that which can be explained.
I sing your astronomical and tender heart,
of French playing-cards, unwounded.

I sing the pain of the statue that you hunt without mercy,
the fear of feeling that awaits you in the street.
I sing the siren nature of the sea that sings of you
on a bicycle of shells and coral.

But before all else I sing a common thought
that unites us in the dark and golden hours.
Art isn't the light that blinds our eyes.
It's first of all love, friendship, fencing.

Es primero que el cuadro que paciente dibujas
el seno de Teresa, la de cutis insomne,
el apretado bucle de Matilde la ingrata,
nuestra amistad pintada como un juego de oca.

Huellas dactilográficas de sangre sobre el oro
rayen el corazón de Cataluña eterna.
Estrellas como puños sin halcón te relumbren,
mientras que tu pintura y tu vida florecen.

No mires la clepsidra con alas membranosas,
ni la dura guadaña de las alegorías.
Viste y desnuda siempre tu pincel en el aire,
frente a la mar poblada con barcos y marinos.

[publicada en *Revista de Occidente*, Madrid, abril 1926]

It's first of all the picture that you patiently sketch,
Teresa's breast, she of the sleepless skin,
the tight curl of ungrateful Matilda,
our friendship painted like a game of goose.

Let the dactylographic prints of blood on the gold
scratch the heart of eternal Cataluña.
Let stars like fists without a falcon shine on you,
while your life and painting prosper.

Don't think of the water-clock with membranous wings,
nor the allegories' hard scythe.
You saw, always naked, your paint-brush in the air,
before the sea full of ships and sailors.

[published in *Revista de Occidente*, Madrid, April 1926]

GYPSY BALLADS

ROMANCERO GITANO

1924-1927

GYPSY BALLADS

Lorca's *Romancero Gitano* (1928) was one of the most popular books of poetry ever published in Spain. For the rest of his life and beyond he was stuck with the image of a gypsy poet, and several of the ballads in it are extremely famous.

There had been several gypsy families in the village where he grew up and he had always admired their music and dancing, and sympathised with their position as outsiders. 'The ballads appear to have several different protagonists,' he wrote later. 'But in fact there is only one: Granada...Although it is called Gypsy, the book as a whole is the poem of Andalucía, and I call it Gypsy because the Gypsy is the most distinguished, profound and aristocratic element of my country, the one most representative of its way of being and which best preserves the fire, blood and alphabet of Andalucian and universal truth...There is just one protagonist, Anguish, great and dark as a summer's sky.' The word for anguish is *pena*, stressed so heavily in 'Ballad of the Black Sorrow', and the book is dominated by tragic figures like Soledad and Amargo, discussed in more detail on page 16.

Do not expect these ballads to tell a straightforward story. They may do so ('The Fight', 'The Faithless Wife'), but more often the reader is left to puzzle out the meaning and in some cases this cannot be done.

The poet is obsessed with the passion and violence which he senses just below the surface of Spanish society. Himself neither a fighter nor a ladies' man, he writes about how the Spanish male is expected to be both these things – like the gypsy in 'The Faithless Wife' who is 'almost compelled' to make love, Tony Camborio, and the rival gangs in 'The Fight'.

'The book begins with two invented myths,' Lorca wrote, 'the moon as a deathly ballerina and the wind as a satyr.' The first poem shows a typical Lorca landscape – moon, wind, horseman, olive trees, innocent child – and suggests that the gypsies are violent (they want to cut out the moon's heart) but also victims (they are weeping in the last verse). These themes will reappear. 'Preciosa and the Wind' concerns the attempted rape of a young girl and suggests the great violence of natural forces, whether the wind or sexual passion. It is inspired by Greek legends about the god Pan, but in this poem the girl is not changed into a tree but takes refuge with the slightly comic figure of the English consul – presumably in Gibraltar.

'The Fight' is about a vendetta between rival gypsy gangs, and suggests pessimistically that killing is a constant factor in human life and has been going on ever since the Romans occupied Spain. Albacete is a southern town which manufactured switchblades. 'Iris' (*lirio*) is a word which Lorca uses to suggest wounds, as later in the *Lament for Ignacio Sánchez Mejías*.

Lorca himself said that in 'Somnambular Ballad'…'no one knows what is happening, not even me'. Robert G. Havard, in an interesting essay, compares it to a dream of which fragments are vividly remembered but which doesn't tell a coherent story. Who is the girl on the balcony, is she dead at the end of the poem, why is the young man wounded (a smuggler?) and who is the friend who will not shelter him? We don't know, but we can be sure that this too is a poem about bloodshed and that the 'drunken Civil Guards' introduce an ominous note. Some of the images are very traditional ('the ship upon the sea and the horse on the mountain'), yet at the same time it has the baffling quality of so much avant-garde art.

'The Gypsy Nun', like 'The Spinster at Mass' (page 45), shows the tension between Catholic rituals and human instincts. 'The Faithless Wife', which very soon became notorious, was inspired by a traditional Andalucían ballad. Lorca's brother Francisco tells us that they once heard a mule driver sing the lines:

> So I took her to the river
> thinking that she was a maiden,
> but she had a husband.

'Some time later, one day when we were speaking of the ballad "The Faithless Wife", I reminded Federico of the mule driver's song. To my enormous surprise, he had completely forgotten it. He thought the first three lines of the ballad were as much his as the rest of the poem. More than that, I thought I could tell that he did not like my insistence, for he continued to believe that I was mistaken.' He certainly succeeded in transforming a scrap of folksong into a brilliant and popular poem on a universal theme.

There follow three poems about archangels, popular figures among the common people, and the three cities of Andalucía with which he associates them. St Michael had a chapel on a hill in Granada which pilgrims used to climb on the saint's feast day. His statue was dressed in petticoats by the pious and, like St Gabriel, he is an erotic rather than a religious figure. He is 'Berber' just as St Raphael is 'Moorish', and this suggests that popular religion in this part of Spain has been influenced by the Arabs.

'St Raphael' is another poem which is difficult to interpret, referring less to the archangel than to the city's Roman past. 'St Gabriel' is mildly blasphemous, using the Annunciation legend to suggest that the pregnant gypsy girl is passionately in love with the saint. The Giralda is a Moorish tower in Sevilla. All three poems are steeped in local imagery and this is what dwells in the reader's mind; none has a traditional narrative.

There follow two poems about Antonito (Tony) Camborio, whom Lorca described as 'a true gypsy, incapable of evil'. Like St Gabriel he is young, handsome and sexually desirable, but not 'manly'. In 'The Arrest', his fellow gypsies despise him because he does not resist the hated Civil Guard, wearers of three-cornered hats. The knives which were such important symbols in 'The Fight' are now 'old' and buried. But they come back with a vengeance in the next poem in which he is killed by his cousins, perhaps as a punishment for not being "normal". The poet quite obviously feels an affinity with him because he is made to call 'Federico García' in his agony.

The 'Ballad of the Spanish Civil Guard' may have had its roots in an incident of 1919 when Lorca saw two gypsies who had been arrested and then beaten up by them. The *benemérita* – policemen who patrol the roads – were very much hated by the Spanish poor, as Arturo Barea explains:

> This is Spain – an enormous barracks of the Civil Guard. They are black, they, their horses, the horseshoes of their horses. Black means mourning. Everything in Spain is black. The Civil Guard are the keepers of this black soul of Spain. Their capes get stained with ink, the ink that runs out of the horn inkwells they use, filling in official reports which inundate Spain and stock her prisons. Their capes are stained with wax...They are killers...Their brains, their minds, their skulls are full of the idea of killing...They ride by night...Therefore people walk on tiptoes wherever the Civil Guard go; they fall silent and walk as though on rubber tyres.

They were to become one of the main props of Franco's regime. By contrast the gypsies in their dream-city (Jerez de la Frontera, an Andalucían town which is the home of sherry) stand for innocent pleasure and the power of the imagination. But the Virgin and St Joseph of their childlike faith cannot protect them, and the badly wounded horse, like the one in Picasso's *Guernica*, suggests that natural vitality is helpless against organised violence.

The Right was offended by this poem, of course. Only a few weeks before the Civil War someone denounced it to the prosecutor and Lorca had to visit the local courthouse to explain what it was about. The Civil Guard were suspected of being responsible for his murder. In fact they were not, yet the poem does read like an uncanny forecast of what was to come.

'Thamar and Amnón' is based on the Old Testament legend (2 Samuel 13) about the rape of a sister by her brother. In the Biblical version Amnon, King David's son, pretends to be ill and violates Thamar when she comes to his room to nurse him. It had frequently been re-used in Spanish literature, the hot landscape in which it occurs sounds Spanish, and the poem is one of enormous power and intensity.

Lorca was not entirely pleased with the reputation this book brought him. 'The gypsies are nothing but a theme,' he wrote. 'I could just as well be the poet of sewing needles or hydraulic landscapes. Furthermore, this "gypsy" business gives me an uneducated, uncultured tone and makes me into a "savage poet", which you know I am not.' Perhaps this accounts for his radical change of style in his next volume, *Poet in New York*.

In the Spanish, every other line ends on a strong vowel-sound, *a*, *e*, *i* or *o*. This is quite untranslatable. I have used rhyme or half-rhyme where it seemed appropriate, but in most cases the poem dictates its own form.

C

Romance de la luna, luna

La luna vino a la fragua
con su polisón de nardos.
El niño la mira mira.
El niño la está mirando.
En el aire conmovido
mueve la luna sus brazos
y enseña, lúbrica y pura,
sus senos de duro estaño.
Huye luna, luna, luna.
Si vinieran los gitanos,
harían con tu corazón
collares y anillos blancos.
Niño, déjame que baile.
Cuando vengan los gitanos,
te encontrarán sobre el yunque
con los ojillos cerrados.
Huye luna, luna, luna,
que ya siento sus caballos.
Niño, déjame, no pises
mi blancor almidonado.

El jinete se acercaba
tocando el tambor del llano.
Dentro de la fragua el niño,
tiene los ojos cerrados.

Por el olivar venían,
bronce y sueño, los gitanos.
Las cabezas levantadas
y los ojos entornados.

¡Cómo canta la zumaya,
ay cómo canta en el árbol!
Por el cielo va la luna
con un niño de la mano.

Dentro de la fragua lloran,
dando gritos, los gitanos.
El aire la vela, vela.
El aire la está velando.

Ballad of the Moon, Moon

The moon came to the smithy
with her bustle of white rose.
The child looks at her,
and looks, and looks.
In the agitated air
the moon moves her arm
and shows, pure, shameless,
her breasts of hard tin.
'Run away, moon, moon, moon.
If the gypsies come,
they'll twist your heart to necklaces
and rings of white stone.'
'Child, let me dance.
When the gypsies come,
they'll find you, little eyes closed,
on the anvil of iron.'
'Run away, moon, moon, moon,
for now I hear their horses.'
'Leave me, child, do not tread
upon my starchy whiteness.'

The horseman was approaching
drumming on the plain.
Inside the forge the child
closed his eyes again.

Through the olive grove the gypsies came,
dream and bronze.
Their heads held high
and their eyes half-closed.

Ah, how the owl sings!
how it sings in the tree!
Holding a child's hand
the moon walks through the sky.

Inside the forge the gypsies
shout and weep.
The wind is watching over it,
watching over it.

Preciosa y el aire

Su luna de pergamino
Preciosa tocando viene
por un anfibio sendero
de cristales y laureles.
El silencio sin estrellas,
huyendo del sonsonete,
cae donde el mar bate y canta
su noche llena de peces.
En los picos de la sierra
los carabineros duermen
guardando las blancas torres
donde viven los ingleses.
Y los gitanos del agua
levantan por distraerse,
glorietas de caracolas
y ramas de pino verde.

*

Su luna de pergamino
Preciosa tocando viene.
Al verla se ha levantado
el viento, que nunca duerme.
San Cristobalón desnudo,
lleno de lenguas celestes,
mira a la niña tocando
una dulce gaita ausente.

Niña, deja que levante
tu vestido para verte.
Abre en mis dedos antiguos
la rosa azul de tu vientre.

Preciosa tira el pandero
y corre sin detenerse.
El viento-hombrón la persigue
con una espada caliente.

Preciosa and the Wind

Beating her moon of parchment,
Preciosa comes,
walking an amphibious path
of laurels and of glass.
The starless silence falls
to escape from her jangling
to where the dark and fish-filled sea
is beating and singing.
In the peaks of the sierra
the sentries sleep,
guarding the white towers
where the English live.
And the water-gypsies
build, to pass the time,
summer-houses made of shells
and branches of green pine.

*

Beating her moon of parchment,
Preciosa comes.
The wind gets up to see her,
the wind who never sleeps.
St Christopher, naked
and full of heavenly tongues,
looks at the girl playing
a sweet and absent song.

'Girl, let me see you,
let me lift up your clothes.
Open to my old fingers
your womb's blue rose.'

Preciosa drops her tambourine
and runs without pausing.
After her, with his hot sword,
comes the wind-man.

Frunce su rumor el mar.
Los olivos palidecen.
Cantan las flautas de umbría
y el liso gong de la nieve.

    ¡Preciosa, corre, Preciosa,
que te coge el viento verde!
¡Preciosa, corre, Preciosa!
¡Míralo por donde viene!
Sátiro de estrellas bajas
con sus lenguas relucientes.

                    *

    Preciosa, llena de miedo,
entra en la casa que tiene,
más arriba de los pinos,
el cónsul de los ingleses.

    Asustados por los gritos
tres carabineros vienen,
sus negras capas ceñidas
y los gorros en las sienes.

    El inglés da a la gitana
un vaso de tibia leche,
y una copa de ginebra
que Preciosa no se bebe.

    Y mientras cuenta, llorando,
su aventura a aquella gente,
en las tejas de pizarra
el viento, furioso, muerde.

Reyerta

En la mitad del barranco
las navajas de Albacete,
bellas de sangre contraria,
relucen como los peces.

The sea wrinkles its sound.
The olives go grey.
The flutes of the shade sing
and the snow's smooth gong.

Preciosa, run, Preciosa,
lest the green wind catch you!
Preciosa, run, Preciosa!
Look where he comes!
Satyr of low stars
with their tongues gleaming.

                    *

Preciosa, full of fear,
goes into the house,
high above the pines,
of the English consul.

Startled by her cries
there appear three sentries,
their black clothes belted
and caps on their temples.

The consul gives the gypsy
a tumbler of warm milk,
also a glass of gin
Preciosa doesn't drink.

And while she tells them, weeping,
about her adventure,
the wind gnaws the slates
of the roof. He's furious.

The Fight

In the middle of the gulch
the Albacete knives
gleam like fishes, beautiful
with blood of enemies.

Una dura luz de naipe
recorta en el agrio verde,
caballos enfurecidos
y perfiles de jinetes.
En la copa de un olivo
lloran dos viejas mujeres.
El toro de la reyerta
se sube por las paredes.
Angeles negros traían
pañuelos y agua de nieve.
Angeles con grandes alas
de navajas de Albacete.
Juan Antonio el de Montilla
rueda muerto la pendiente,
su cuerpo lleno de lirios
y una granada en las sienes.
Ahora monta cruz de fuego,
carretera de la muerte.

*

El juez, con guardia civil,
por los olivares viene.
Sangre resbalada gime
muda canción de serpiente.
Señores guardias civiles:
aquí pasó lo de siempre.
Han muerto cuatro romanos
y cinco cartagineses.

*

La tarde loca de higueras
y de rumores calientes
cae desmayada en los muslos
heridos de los jinetes.
Y ángeles negros volaban
por el aire del poniente.
Angeles de largas trenzas
y corazones de aceite.

A hard light, like playing-cards,
outlines on sour green
infuriated horses
and the profiles of the men.
In the crown of an olive
two old women weep.
Up the walls is climbing
the bull of the fight.
Dark angels carried melted
snow and handkerchieves.
Angels with great wings
of Albacete knives.
Juan Antonio of Montilla
rolls down the slope dead,
his body full of iris,
pomegranate on his head.
Now he rides a fiery cross
along death's high road.

*

The judge, with the Civil Guard
comes through the olive grove.
A quiet song is moaning from
the snake of sliding blood.
'Gentlemen of the Civil Guard,
it's the same tale always.
Here we have four Romans dead
and five Carthaginians.'

*

The afternoon, mad with hot
rumours, and fig trees,
faints across the horsemen's
lacerated thighs.
And dark angels flew
through the air of the west.
Angels with long hair
and olive-oil hearts.

Romance sonámbulo

Verde que te quiero verde.
Verde viento. Verdes ramas.
El barco sobre la mar
y el caballo en la montaña.
Con la sombra en la cintura
ella sueña en su baranda,
verde carne, pelo verde,
con ojos de fría plata.
Verde que te quiero verde.
Bajo la luna gitana,
las cosas la están mirando
y ella no puede mirarlas.

                    *

    Verde que te quiero verde.
Grandes estrellas de escarcha,
vienen con el pez de sombra
que abre el camino del alba.
La higuera frota su viento
con la lija de sus ramas,
y el monte, gato garduño,
eriza sus pitas agrias.
¿Pero quién vendrá? ¿Y por dónde…?
Ella sigue en su baranda,
verde carne, pelo verde,
soñando en la mar amarga.

                    *

    Compadre, quiero cambiar
mi caballo por su casa,
mi montura por su espejo,
mi cuchillo por su manta.
Compadre, vengo sangrando,
desde los puertos de Cabra.
Si yo pudiera, mocito,
este trato se cerraba.
Pero yo ya no soy yo.
Ni mi casa es ya mi casa.

Somnambular Ballad

Green how much I want you green.
Green wind. Green branches.
The ship upon the sea
and the horse on the mountain.
With the shadow at her waist
she dreams on her balcony,
green flesh, green hair,
and eyes of cold silver.
Green how much I want you green.
Beneath the gypsy moon,
things are looking at her
and she cannot see them.

*

Green how much I want you green.
Great stars of frost come
with the fish of shadow
that clears the way for dawn.
The fig tree rubs the wind
with its sandpaper branches,
the mountain, like a thieving cat,
bristles with sour plants.
But who will come? And where from...?
She lingers on her balcony,
green flesh, green hair,
dreams of the bitter sea.

*

'My friend, I want to barter
my horse for your house,
my saddle for your looking-glass,
my knife for your blanket.
Friend, I come bleeding
from the passes of Cabra.'
'If I could, young man,
this bargain would be closed.
But I am not myself now,
my house is not my house.'

Compadre, quiero morir
decentemente en mi cama.
De acero, si puede ser,
con las sábanas de holanda.
¿No veis la herida que tengo
desde el pecho a la garganta?
Trescientas rosas morenas
lleva tu pechera blanca.
Tu sangre rezuma y huele
alrededor de tu faja.
Pero yo ya no soy yo.
Ni mi casa es ya mi casa.
Dejadme subir al menos
hasta las altas barandas,
¡dejadme subir!, dejadme
hasta las verdes barandas.
Barandales de la luna
por donde retumba el agua.

                    *

    Ya suben los dos compadres
hacia las altas barandas.
Dejando un rastro de sangre.
Dejando un rastro de lágrimas.
Temblaban en los tejados
farolillos de hojalata.
Mil panderos de cristal,
herían la madrugada.

                    *

    Verde que te quiero verde,
verde viento, verdes ramas.
Los dos compadres subieron.
El largo viento, dejaba
en la boca un raro gusto
de hiel, de menta y de albahaca.
¡Compadre! ¿Dónde está, dime?
¿Dónde está tu niña amarga?
¡Cuántas veces te esperó!
¡Cuántas veces te esperara,
cara fresca, negro pelo,
en esta verde baranda!

                    *

'Friend, I want to die
in my bed and decently.
Made of steel, if possible,
with sheets of fine linen.
Do you not see the wound
from my breast to my throat?'
'Three hundred dark roses
are on your white shirt.
Your blood is pungent
and oozes round your sash.
But I am not myself now,
my house is not my house'.
'Let me climb up, at least,
to the high balustrades,
let me climb! let me,
to the green balustrades.
Balustrades of the moon
where the water resounds.'

                    *

Now the two friends are climbing
to the high balustrades.
Leaving a trail of blood.
Leaving a trail of tears.
On the roofs trembled
little tin lanterns.
A thousand glass tambourines
wounded the dawn.

                    *

Green how much I want you green,
green wind, green branches.
The two friends climbed up.
The great wind left a strange
taste of gall in the mouth,
of mint and of basil.
'Friend! Tell me, where is she,
where is your bitter girl?
How often she waited for you!
How often she will wait,
fresh face, dark hair,
on this green balustrade!'

                    *

Sobre el rostro del aljibe,
se mecía la gitana.
Verde carne, pelo verde,
con ojos de fría plata.
Un carámbano de luna
la sostiene sobre el agua.
La noche se puso íntima
como una pequeña plaza.
Guardias civiles borrachos
en la puerta golpeaban.
Verde que te quiero verde.
Verde viento. Verdes ramas.
El barco sobre la mar.
Y el caballo en la montaña.

La monja gitana

Silencio de cal y mirto.
Malvas en las hierbas finas.
La monja borda alhelíes
sobre una tela pajiza.
Vuelan en la araña gris,
siete pájaros del prisma.
La iglesia gruñe a lo lejos
como un oso panza arriba.
¡Qué bien borda! ¡Con qué gracia!
Sobre la tela pajiza,
ella quisiera bordar
flores de su fantasía.
¡Qué girasol! ¡Qué magnolia
de lentejuelas y cintas!
¡Qué azafranes y qué lunas,
en el mantel de la misa!
Cinco toronjas se endulzan
en la cercana cocina.
Las cinco llagas de Cristo
cortadas en Almería.
Por los ojos de la monja
galopan dos caballistas.

Above the tank's surface
the gypsy was swaying.
Green flesh, green hair,
and eyes of cold silver.
An icicle of moon
holds her over the water.
The night became intimate
as a small square.
Drunken Civil Guards
were beating the door down.
Green how much I want you green.
Green wind. Green branches.
The ship upon the sea.
And the horse on the mountain.

The Gypsy Nun

Silence of lime and myrtle.
Mallows in the fine grass.
The nun embroiders wallflowers
on a straw-coloured cloth.
Seven prismatic birds fly
in the grey chandelier.
The church growls far off
like an overthrown bear.
How well she embroiders!
How gracefully!
On the yellow cloth, she'd like to sew
flowers of fantasy.
Sunflower! Magnolia
of sequins and ribbons!
On the altar-cloth,
such moons, such saffrons!
In the kitchen nearby
five grapefruits grow sweet.
Five nasturtiums in Almeria
cut.
Through the eyes of the nun
two horsemen gallop.

Un rumor último y sordo
le despega la camisa,
y al mirar nubes y montes
en las yertas lejanías,
se quiebra su corazón
de azúcar y yerbaluisa.
¡Oh!, qué llanura empinada
con veinte soles arriba.
¡Qué ríos puestos de pie
vislumbra su fantasía!
Pero sigue con sus flores,
mientras que de pie, en la brisa,
la luz juega el ajedrez
alto de la celosía.

La casada infiel

Y que yo me la llevé al río
creyendo que era mozuela,
pero tenía marido.
Fue la noche de Santiago
y casi por compromiso.
Se apagaron los faroles
y se encendieron los grillos.
En las últimas esquinas
toqué sus pechos dormidos,
y se me abrieron de pronto
como ramos de jacintos.
El almidón de su enagua
me sonaba en el oído,
como una pieza de seda
rasgada por diez cuchillos.
Sin luz de plata en sus copas
los árboles han crecido,
y un horizonte de perros
ladra muy lejos del río.

*

A remote, dull sound lifts
her petticoat.
As she stares at the stiff, distant
hills and clouds,
her heart of verbena
and sugar, breaks.
What a lofty plain,
with twenty suns!
What upstanding rivers
her fantasy forms!
But she sews her flowers still,
while, in the breeze,
on the high lattice-window
the light plays chess.

The Faithless Wife

So I took her to the river
thinking that she was a maiden
but she had a husband.
It was on St James's night
and almost in duty bound.
The lanterns went out
and the crickets lit up.
At the last street corners
I touched her sleeping breasts,
and, suddenly, they opened
like a hyacinth's spikes.
The starch of her petticoat
sounded in my ears
like a fragment of silk
ripped by ten knives.
Away from the silver light
the trees had grown larger,
a horizon of dogs barked
very far from the river.

*

Pasadas las zarzamoras,
los juncos y los espinos,
bajo su mata de pelo
hice un hoyo sobre el limo.
Yo me quité la corbata.
Ella se quitó el vestido.
Yo el cinturón con revólver.
Ella sus cuatro corpiños.
Ni nardos ni caracolas
tienen el cutis tan fino,
ni los cristales con luna
relumbran con ese brillo.
Sus muslos se me escapaban
como peces sorprendidos,
la mitad llenos de lumbre,
la mitad llenos de frío.
Aquella noche corrí
el mejor de los caminos,
montado en potra de nácar
sin bridas y sin estribos.
No quiero decir, por hombre,
las cosas que ella me dijo.
La luz del entendimiento
me hace ser muy comedido.
Sucia de besos y arena,
yo me la llevé del río.
Con el aire se batían
las espadas de los lirios.

Me porté como quien soy.
Como un gitano legítimo.
La regalé un costurero
grande de raso pajizo,
y no quise enamorarme
porque teniendo marido
me dijo que era mozuela
cuando la llevaba al río.

82

Going past the blackberries,
the hawthorns and the reeds
underneath her bush of hair
I hollowed out the sand.
I took off my tie.
She took off her dress.
I, my revolver belt.
And she, her four bodices.
Not a tuberose nor a shell
has skin as fine as hers,
nor do crystals in the moon
shine with such brilliance.
Her thighs slipped away from me
like startled fishes,
one half full of flame
the other of coldness.
That night I galloped
along the best of roads
on a mother-of-pearl filly
without stirrups or bridles.
As a man, the things she said
to me I won't repeat.
The light of understanding
has made me most discreet.
Smeared with kisses and with sand
I took her from the river.
The swords of the iris
were battling with the air.

I behaved like what I am.
Like a proper gypsy.
I gave her a big sewing box
of straw-coloured satin.
I didn't want to fall in love,
for, though she had a husband,
she said she was a maiden
when I took her to the river.

Romance de la pena negra

Las piquetas de los gallos
cavan buscando la aurora,
cuando por el monte oscuro
baja Soledad Montoya.
Cobre amarillo, su carne,
huele a caballo y a sombra.
Yunques ahumados sus pechos,
gimen canciones redondas.
Soledad: ¿por quién preguntas
sin compaña y a estas horas?
Pregunte por quien pregunte,
dime: ¿a ti qué se te importa?
Vengo a buscar lo que busco,
mi alegría y mi persona.
Soledad de mis pesares,
caballo que se desboca,
al fin encuentra la mar
y se lo tragan las olas.
No me recuerdes el mar,
que la pena negra, brota
en las tierras de aceituna
bajo el rumor de las hojas.
¡Soledad, qué pena tienes!
¡Qué pena tan lastimosa!
Lloras zumo de limón
agrio de espera y de boca.
¡Qué pena tan grande! Corro
mi casa como una loca,
mis dos trenzas por el suelo,
de la cocina a la alcoba.
¡Qué pena! Me estoy poniendo
de azabache, carne y ropa.
¡Ay mis camisas de hilo!
¡Ay mis muslos de amapola!
Soledad: lava tu cuerpo
con agua de las alondras,
y deja tu corazón
en paz, Soledad Montoya.

*

Ballad of the Black Sorrow

Beaks of the cockerels delve,
searching for the dawn,
when down the dark mountain
comes Soledad Montoya.
Her flesh, like brass, smells
of horse and of shadow.
Her breasts, smoky anvils,
lament rounded songs.
'Soledad, whom do you ask for,
alone, at this hour?'
'Whoever I ask for,
what business of yours?
I search for what I search for,
myself and my joy.'
'Soledad of my sorrows,
when a horse runs away,
it finds the sea at last
and is swallowed by waves.'
'Don't tell me of the sea,
for the black sorrow rises
beneath the murmur of leaves
in the country of olives.'
'Soledad, how sad you are!
What pitiful grief!
You weep drops of lemon,
long-stored, sour in the mouth.'
'Such great sorrow! I run
through my house like one mad,
my two tresses sweep the floor
from kitchen to bed.
Such sorrow! My flesh and clothes
are turning to jet.
Ah, my white linen petticoats,
thighs poppy red!'
'Soledad, wash your body
with water of skylarks.
And let your heart be at peace,
Soledad Montoya.'

*

Por abajo canta el río:
volante de cielo y hojas.
Con flores de calabaza,
la nueva luz se corona.
¡Oh pena de los gitanos!
Pena limpia y siempre sola.
¡Oh pena de cauce oculto
y madrugada remota!

San Miguel
(Granada)

Se ven desde las barandas,
por el monte, monte, monte,
mulos y sombras de mulos
cargados de girasoles.

   Sus ojos en las umbrías
se empañan de inmensa noche.
En los recodos del aire,
cruje la aurora salobre.

   Un cielo de mulos blancos
cierra sus ojos de azogue
dando a la quieta penumbra
un final de corazones.
Y el agua se pone fría
para que nadie la toque.
Agua loca y descubierta
por el monte, monte, monte.

                    *

   San Miguel lleno de encajes
en la alcoba de su torre,
enseña sus bellos muslos
ceñidos por los faroles.

Down below sings the river,
flying through sky and leaves.
With flowers of the pumpkin
the new light makes crowns.
Oh, sadness of the gypsies!
Pure pain, always alone.
Pain of the hidden water course
and the far-distant dawn.

St Michael
(Granada)

From the balconies you see
mules and shadows of mules
go through the mountain, mountain, mountain,
weighed down with sunflowers.

In the shade their eyes cloud over
with enormous night.
In the elbows of the air
crackles a dawn of salt.

A sky of white mules closes
its quicksilver eyes,
gives to the calm penumbra
an ending-place of hearts.
And the water turns cold
so that no one may touch it.
From the mountain, mountain, mountain,
water mad and naked.

                    *

St Michael in his tower room,
wrapped in lace,
reveals, ringed by lanterns,
his beautiful thighs.

Arcángel domesticado
en el gesto de las doce,
finge una cólera dulce
de plumas y ruiseñores.
San Miguel canta en los vidrios;
efebo de tres mil noches,
fragante de agua colonia
y lejano de las flores.

*

El mar baila por la playa,
un poema de balcones.
Las orillas de la luna
pierden juncos, ganan voces.
Vienen manolas comiendo
semillas de girasoles,
los culos grandes y ocultos
como planetas de cobre.
Vienen altos caballeros
y damas de triste porte,
morenas por la nostalgia
de un ayer de ruiseñores.
Y el obispo de Manila,
ciego de azafrán y pobre,
dice misa con dos filos
para mujeres y hombres.

*

San Miguel se estaba quieto
en la alcoba de su torre,
con las enaguas cuajadas
de espejitos y entredoses.

San Miguel, rey de los globos
y de los números nones,
en el primor berberisco
de gritos y miradores.

Tamed archangel
pointing up to the twelve,
pretends a sweet anger
of feathers, nightingales.
Youth of three thousand nights,
St Michael sings in the glass,
fragrant with cologne,
far away from the flowers.

*

The sea dances a poem
of balconies.
The shores of the moon
gain voices, lose reeds.
Flashy girls come, chewing
seeds of sunflower,
their large bottoms hidden
like planets of copper.
Tall horsemen come
and sad-looking women,
for yesterday's nightingales
dark with yearning.
And the bishop of Manila,
poor, blind with saffron,
says a double-edged mass
for men and women.

*

St Michael in his tower room
stayed quiet,
his petticoats crusted
with sequins and ruffles.

St Michael, king of the spheres,
and lord of odd numbers.
Shouting. Closed balconies.
Beauty of Berbers.

San Rafael

(Córdoba)

I

Coches cerrados llegaban
a las orillas le juncos
donde las ondas alisan
romano torso desnudo.
Coches, que el Guadalquivir
tiende en su cristal maduro,
entre láminas de flores
y resonancias de nublos.
Los niños tejen y cantan
el desengaño del mundo,
cerca de los viejos coches
perdidos en el nocturno.
Pero Córdoba no tiembla
bajo el misterio confuso,
pues si la sombra levanta
la arquitectura del humo,
un pie de mármol afirma
su casto fulgor enjuto.
Pétalos de lata débil
recaman los grises puros
de la brisa, desplegada
sobre los arcos de triunfo.
Y mientras el puente sopla
diez rumores de Neptuno,
vendedores de tabaco
huyen por el roto muro.

II

Un solo pez en el agua
que a las dos Córdobas junta:
Blanda Córdoba de juncos.
Córdoba de arquitectura.
Niños de cara impasible
en la orilla se desnudan,
aprendices de Tobías
y Merlines de cintura,

St Raphael

(Córdoba)

I

Closed coaches were arriving
at the edges of the reeds
where a naked Roman torso
is polished by the waves.
Coaches that Guadalquivir
spreads in her mellow glass,
held between sheets of flowers
and the echoes of the clouds.
The children weave and sing
the world's disillusionment,
close to the ancient coaches
lost in the depths of night.
But Córdoba doesn't tremble
in that strange mystery,
for if the shadow raises
the smoky shapes, you see
a marble foot, affirming
its chaste dry brilliance.
Petals of feeble tin
embroider the pure greys
of the wind, which spreads itself
above triumphal arches.
And while the bridge is whispering
ten rumours about Neptune,
tobacco sellers flee
along the broken wall.

II

A single fish in the water
makes two Córdobas one:
Smooth Córdoba of rushes.
Córdoba made of stone.
Children without expression
strip naked on the bank,
apprentices of Tobías
and Merlins of the waist,

para fastidiar al pez
en irónica pregunta
si quiere flores de vino
o saltos de media luna.
Pero el pez que dora el agua
y los mármoles enluta,
les da lección y equilibrio
de solitaria columna.
El Arcángel aljamiado
de lentejuelas oscuras,
en el mitin de las ondas
buscaba rumor y cuna.

*

Un solo pez en el agua.
Dos Córdobas de hermosura.
Córdoba quebrada en chorros.
Celeste Córdoba enjuta.

San Gabriel
(Sevilla)

I

Un bello niño de junco,
anchos hombros, fino talle,
piel de nocturna manzana,
boca triste y ojos grandes,
nervio de plata caliente
ronda la desierta calle.
Sus zapatos de charol
rompen las dalias del aire,
con los dos ritmos que cantan
breves lutos celestiales.
En la ribera del mar
no hay palma que se le iguale,
ni emperador coronado
ni lucero caminante.

and ask an ironic question
to torment the fish,
'does it want flowers made of wine
or the half moon's gaps?'
But the fish, that gilds the water
and makes the marble mourn,
teaches them of the balance
of an isolated column.
The Moorish archangel
of dark spangles, seeks
for rumour and for cradle
at the meeting place of waves.

                    *

A single fish in the water.
Two Córdobas of beauty.
One broken into streams.
One heavenly and dry.

St Gabriel
(Sevilla)

      I

A handsome willowy youth,
broad shoulders, slender waist,
skin of a midnight apple,
sad mouth and great eyes,
with the vigour of hot silver
roams the deserted street.
His patent leather shoes
crush dahlias underfoot,
with two rhythms that sing
of short celestial grief.
No palm tree can compare
with him, on the sea shore,
nor yet a crowned emperor
or wandering star.

Cuando la cabeza inclina
sobre su pecho de jaspe,
la noche busca llanuras
porque quiere arrodillarse.
Las guitarras suenan solas
para San Gabriel Arcángel,
domador de palomillas
y enemigo de los sauces.
San Gabriel: El niño llora
en el vientre de su madre.
No olvides que los gitanos
te regalaron el traje.

II

Anunciación de los Reyes,
bien lunada y mal vestida,
abre la puerta al lucero
que por la calle venía.
El Arcángel San Gabriel,
entre azucena y sonrisa,
biznieto de la Giralda,
se acercaba de visita.
En su chaleco bordado
grillos ocultos palpitan.
Las estrellas de la noche
se volvieron campanillas.
San Gabriel: aquí me tienes
con tres clavos de alegría.
Tu fulgor abre jazmines
sobre mi cara encendida.
Dios te salves Anunciación.
Morena de maravilla.
Tendrás un niño más bello
que los tallos de la brisa.
¡Ay San Gabriel de mis ojos!
¡Gabrielillo de mi vida!,
para sentarte yo sueño
un sillón de clavellinas.
Dios te salve, Anunciación,
bien lunada y mal vestida.
Tu niño tendrá en el pecho
un lunar y tres heridas.

94

When his head inclines
on his jasper breast,
the night looks round for prairies
to fall upon her knees.
The guitars strike singly
for St Gabriel Archangel,
tamer of moths
and enemy of the willow.
'St Gabriel,' the child cries
in his mother's belly.
'Don't forget that your suit
was a gift from the gypsies.'

II

Anunciación de los Reyes,
well favoured, poorly dressed,
leaves her door open for the star
who's coming down the street.
St Gabriel Archangel
between lily and smile,
great-grandson of Giralda's tower
was paying her a visit.
In his embroidered waistcoat
throbbed hidden crickets.
The stars of the night
became little bells.
'St Gabriel: Here I am,
three shafts of happiness.
Your radiance opens jasmines
upon my blushing face.'
'God save you, Anunciación.
Dark girl of miracle.
You will bear a child fairer
than the stems of the breeze.'
'Ah, St Gabriel, my eyesight!
Little Gabriel of my life!
I dream, for you to sit upon,
a throne of pink carnations.'
'God save you, Anunciación,
well favoured, poorly dressed.
Your child shall bear a blemish
and three wounds upon his chest.'

¡Ay San Gabriel que reluces!
¡Gabrielillo de mi vida!
En el fondo de mis pechos
ya nace la leche tibia.
Dios te salve, Anunciación.
Madre de cien dinastías.
Aridos lucen tus ojos,
paisajes de caballista.

*

El niño canta en el seno
de Anunciación sorprendida.
Tres balas de almendra verde
tiemblan en su vocecita.

Ya San Gabriel en el aire
por una escala subía.
Las estrellas de la noche
se volvieron siemprevivas.

Prendimiento de Antoñito el Camborio en el camino de Sevilla

Antonio Torres Heredia,
hijo y nieto de Camborios,
con una vara de mimbre
va a Sevilla a ver los toros.
Moreno de verde luna
anda despacio y garboso.
Sus empavonados bucles
le brillan entre los ojos.
A la mitad del camino
cortó limones redondos,
y los fue tirando al agua
hasta que la puso de oro.
Y a la mitad del camino,
bajo las ramas de un olmo,
guardia civil caminera
lo llevó codo con codo.

*

'Ah, shining St Gabriel!
Little Gabriel of my life!
Deep in my breasts already
is springing the warm milk.'
'God save you, Anunciación.
Mother of a hundred dynasties.
Your eyes shine dry
like the horsemen's landscapes.'

       *

The child sings in the heart
of startled Anunciación.
Three bullets of green almond throb
in his little voice.

Now St Gabriel in the air
was going up a ladder.
The stars became
everlasting flowers.

The Arrest of Tony Camborio
on the Road to Sevilla

Antonio Torres Heredia,
son and grandson of Camborios,
walks with a willow cane
to Sevilla to see the bulls.
Dark from the green moon,
he slowly, gracefully goes.
His shining curls gleam
between his eyes.
Half way through the journey
he picked some round lemons,
and threw them in the water
until it turned golden.
And half way through the journey
beneath an elm,
five Civil Guards
arrested him.

       *

D

El día se va despacio,
la tarde colgada a un hombro,
dando una larga torera
sobre el mar y los arroyos.
Las aceitunas aguardan
la noche de Capricornio,
y una corta brisa, ecuestre,
salta los montes de plomo.
Antonio Torres Heredia,
hijo y nieto de Camborios,
viene sin vara de mimbre
entre los cinco tricornios.

Antonio, ¿quién eres tú?
Si te llamaras Camborio,
hubieras hecho una fuente
de sangre, con cinco chorros.
Ni tú eres hijo de nadie,
ni legítimo Camborio.
¡Se acabaron los gitanos
que iban por el monte solos!
Están los viejos cuchillos
tiritando bajo el polvo.

*

A las nueve de la noche
lo llevan al calabozo,
mientras los guardias civiles
beben limonada todos.
Y a las nueve de la noche
le cierran el calabozo,
mientras el cielo reluce
como la grupa de un potro.

The day recedes slowly,
evening hangs on a shoulder,
making a long feint
across sea and river.
The olives wait
for the Capricorn night,
a small breeze, like a horseman,
jumps hills of lead.
Antonio Torres Heredia,
son and grandson of Camborios,
without his willow cane
walks between five tricorns.

Antonio, what are you?
If you were called Camborio,
you'd have made a fountain
of five blood jets flow.
You are nobody's son,
and not a true Camborio.
Gone are the lonely gypsies
who went upon the mountain!
The old knives under
the dust are shivering.

                         *

At nine o'clock in the evening
he's carried to the jail,
while all the Civil Guards
are drinking lemonade.
And at nine in the evening
his cell is shut
while the sky shines like
the rump of a colt.

Muerte de Antoñito el Camborio

Voces de muerte sonaron
cerca del Guadalquivir.
Voces antiguas que cercan
voz de clavel varonil.
Les clavó sobre las botas
mordiscos de jabalí.
En la lucha daba saltos
jabonados de delfín.
Bañó con sangre enemiga
su corbata carmesí,
pero eran cuatro puñales
y tuvo que sucumbir.
Cuando las estrellas clavan
rejones al agua gris,
cuando los erales sueñan
verónicas de alhelí,
voces de muerte sonaron
cerca del Guadalquivir.

*

Antonio Torres Heredia,
Camborio de dura crin,
moreno de verde luna,
voz de clavel varonil:
¿Quién te ha quitado la vida
cerca del Guadalquivir?
Mis cuatro primos Heredias
hijos de Benamejí.
Lo que en otros no envidiaban,
ya lo envidiaban en mí.
Zapatos color corinto,
medallones de marfil,
y este cutis amasado
con aceituna y jazmín.
¡Ay Antoñito el Camborio,
digno de una Emperatriz!
Acuérdate de la Virgen
porque te vas a morir.

The Death of Tony Camborio

Voices of death resounded
beside the Guadalquivir.
Ancient voices surround
the manly carnation's voice.
Upon their boots he nailed
bites of the wild boar.
In the fight he leapt
as slippery as a dolphin.
In his enemies' blood
he bathed his crimson tie,
but there were four daggers,
he had to die.
When the stars nail spears
upon the grey water,
when the young bulls dream
passes like the wallflower,
voices of death resounded
beside the Guadalquivir.

                    *

– 'Antonio Torres Heredia,
Camborio of hard locks,
dark in the green moon,
the manly carnation's voice:
Who took away your life
beside the Guadalquivir?'
– 'My four Heredias cousins
Benameji's sons.
They did not envy in others
what they envied in me.
My raisin-coloured shoes,
my ivory medallions,
this skin of mine, a blend
of olive and of jasmine.'
– 'Ah, Tony Camborio,
worthy of an Empress!
Think about the Virgin
because you're going to die.'

¡Ay Federico García,
llama a la Guardia Civil!
Ya mi talle se ha quebrado
como caña de maíz.

*

    Tres golpes de sangre tuvo
y se murió de perfil.
Viva moneda que nunca
se volverá a repetir.
Un ángel marchoso pone
su cabeza en un cojín.
Otros de rubor cansado,
encendieron un candil.
Y cuando los cuatro primos
llegan a Benamejí,
voces de muerte cesaron
cerca del Guadalquivir.

Romance del emplazado

¡Mi soledad sin descanso!
Ojos chicos de mi cuerpo
y grandes de mi caballo,
no se cierran por la noche
ni miran al otro lado
donde se aleja tranquilo
un sueño de trece barcos.
Sino que limpios y duros
escuderos desvelados,
mis ojos miran un norte
de metales y peñascos
donde mi cuerpo sin venas
consulta naipes helados.

*

– 'Ah, Federico García,
call the Civil Guard!
My waist is snapped
like a stalk of maize.'

        *

Three gushes of blood
and his profile died.
A living coin, never
to be renewed.
A swaggering angel lays
his head upon a cushion.
Others, tired and blushing,
lit a lamp.
And when the four cousins
arrive at Benamejí,
the deathly voices cease
beside the Guadalquivir.

Ballad of the Doomed Man

My loneliness without rest!
The small eyes of my body,
the large eyes of my horse
never close at night
nor look to the other shore
where quietly recedes
a dream of thirteen boats.
Clean and hard, instead,
my eyes, like wide-awake pageboys,
stare towards a north
of crags and metals
where, veinless, my body scans
playing-cards which are frozen.

        *

Los densos bueyes del agua
embisten a los muchachos
que se bañan en las lunas
de sus cuernos ondulados.
Y los martillos cantaban
sobre los yunques sonámbulos,
el insomnio del jinete
y el insomnio del caballo.

*

El veinticinco de junio
le dijeron a el Amargo:
Ya puedes cortar si gustas
las adelfas de tu patio.
Pinta una cruz en la puerta
y pon tu nombre debajo,
porque cicutas y ortigas
nacerán en tu costado,
y agujas de cal mojada
te morderán los zapatos.
Será de noche, en lo oscuro,
por los montes imantados,
donde los bueyes del agua
beben los juncos soñando.
Pide luces y campanas.
Aprende a cruzar las manos,
y gusta los aires fríos
de metales y peñascos.
Porque dentro de dos meses
yacerás amortajado.

*

Espadón de nebulosa
mueve en el aire Santiago.
Grave silencio, de espalda,
manaba el cielo combado.

*

El veinticinco de junio
abrió sus ojos Amargo,
y el veinticinco de agosto
se tendió para cerrarlos.

The massive oxen of water
crash against the boys
who bathe within the moons
of their waving horns.
And the hammers sing
above somnambular anvils,
the sleeplessness of the rider,
the sleeplessness of the horse.

*

On June the twenty-fifth,
they said to Amargo,
'Now cut the oleanders
in your court, if you like.
Paint a cross on your door
and put your name below it,
because hemlock and nettles
will take root in your side,
and needles of damp lime
will bite into your shoes.
It will be at night,
by dark, through magnetic hills,
where the oxen of water
drink rushes, dreaming.
Ask for lights and for bells.
Learn how to cross your hands
and to taste the chill air
of crags and metals.
Because within two months
you're going to lie in a shroud.'

*

St James moves in the air
his sword of shadow.
A heavy silence flowed
from the bent sky's back.

*

On June the twenty-fifth,
Amargo opened his eyes,
on August the twenty-fifth
he lay down to close them.

Hombres bajaban la calle
para ver al emplazado,
que fijaba sobre el muro
su soledad con descanso.
Y la sábana impecable,
de duro acento romano,
daba equilibrio a la muerte
con las rectas de sus paños.

Romance de la Guardia Civil española

Los caballos negros son.
Las herraduras son negras.
Sobre las capas relucen
manchas de tinta y de cera.
Tienen, por eso no lloran,
de plomo las calaveras.
Con el alma de charol
vienen por la carretera.
Jorobados y nocturnos,
por donde animan ordenan
silencios de goma oscura
y miedos de fina arena.
Pasan, si quieren pasar,
y ocultan en la cabeza
una vaga astronomía
de pistolas inconcretas.

               *

¡Oh ciudad de los gitanos!
En las esquinas banderas.
La luna y la calabaza
con las guindas en conserva.
¡Oh ciudad de los gitanos!
¿Quién te vio y no te recuerda?
Ciudad de dolor y almizcle,
con las torres de canela.

               *

They came along the street
to look at the doomed man,
who fixed upon the wall
his loneliness without rest.
And the spotless sheet
with its hard Roman accent
gave death an equilibrium
by the straight lines of its cloth.

Ballad of the Spanish Civil Guard

Black are their horses.
Black the horses' shoes.
On their cloaks are shining
blobs of ink and wax.
Their skulls are of lead,
which is why they don't weep.
With their patent-leather souls
they come along the street.
Hunchbacked, nocturnal,
where they move they command
silence, like dark rubber,
and fear like fine sand.
They pass, if they want to pass,
and hide in their skulls
a vague astronomy
of shadowy pistols.

                    *

Oh, city of the gypsies!
On the corners, flags.
The moon and the pumpkin
and cherries preserved.
Oh, city of the gypsies!
Who that saw you could forget?
City of sorrow, musk
and cinnamon towers.

                    *

Cuando llegaba la noche,
noche que noche nochera,
los gitanos en sus fraguas
forjaban soles y flechas.
Un caballo malherido,
llamaba a todas las puertas.
Gallos de vidrio cantaban
por Jerez de la Frontera.
El viento, vuelve desnudo
la esquina de la sorpresa,
en la noche platinoche
noche, que noche nochera.

*

La Virgen y Sañ José,
perdieron sus castanuelas,
y buscan a los gitanos
para ver si las encuentran.
La Virgen viene vestida
con un traje de alcaldesa
de papel de chocolate
con los collares de almendras.
San José mueve los brazos
bajo una capa de seda.
Detrás va Pedro Domecq
con tres sultanes de Persia.
La media luna, soñaba
un éxtasis de cigüeña.
Estandartes y faroles
invaden las azoteas.
Por los espejos sollozan
bailarinas sin caderas.
Agua y sombra, sombra y agua
por Jerez de la Frontera.

*

¡Oh ciudad de los gitanos!
En las esquinas banderas.
Apaga tus verdes luces
que viene la benemérita.
¡Oh ciudad de los gitanos!
¿Quien te vio y no te recuerda?

When the night fell,
night that darkened night,
the gypsies in their forges
moulded arrows and suns.
A badly wounded horse
knocked at all the doors.
Glass cocks were singing
through Jerez de la Frontera.
The wind swerved naked
round the corner of surprise,
in the night, the silver night,
night that darkened night.

*

The Virgin and St Joseph
have lost their castanets
and search for the gypsies
to see if they can find them.
The Virgin comes clad
in a mayoress's dress
made of chocolate paper
with almond necklaces.
St Joseph moves his arms
beneath a silken cloak.
Behind go three Persian sultans
and Pedro Domecq.
The half moon was dreaming
an ecstatic stork.
Banners and lanterns
invade the flat roofs.
Sobbing in the mirrors
are hipless dancing girls.
Water, shadow, shadow, water
at Jerez de la Frontera.

*

Oh, city of the gypsies!
On the corners, flags.
Put out your green lights
the Civil Guard is coming.
Oh, city of the gypsies!
Who that saw you could forget?

Dejadla lejos del mar,
sin peines para sus crenchas.

*

Avanzan de dos en fondo
a la ciudad de la fiesta.
Un rumor de siemprevivas
invade las cartucheras.
Avanzan de dos en fondo.
Doble nocturno de tela.
El cielo, se les antoja,
una vitrina de espuelas.

*

La ciudad libre de miedo,
multiplicaba sus puertas.
Cuarenta guardias civiles
entran a saco por ellas.
Los relojes se pararon,
y el coñac de las botellas
se disfrazó de noviembre
para no infundir sospechas.
Un vuelo de gritos largos
se levantó en las veletas.
Los sables cortan las brisas
que los cascos atropellan.
Por las calles de penumbra
huyen las gitanas viejas
con los caballos dormidos
y las orzas de monedas.
Por las calles empinadas
suben las capas siniestras,
dejando detrás fugaces
remolinos de tijeras.

En el portal de Belén
los gitanos se congregan.
San José, lleno de heridas,
amortaja a una doncella.
Tercos fusiles agudos
por toda la noche suenan.

Leave her far from the sea
without combs for her hair.

*

The Guards advance, two abreast,
towards the festive city.
A sound of everlasting flowers
invades the cartridge belts.
The Guards advance, two abreast.
Double dark uniforms.
The sky itself, they fancy,
is a showcase of spurs.

*

The city, unsuspecting,
opened wide its doors.
Forty Civil Guards
came through them to plunder.
The clocks stopped,
and the cognac in the bottles
disguised itself as November
not to rouse suspicion.
A flight of loud shrieks
rose from the weathercocks.
The sabres slash the breezes
trampled by the hooves.
Along the streets of darkness
old gypsy women fled
with their sleepy horses
and crocks full of gold.
Through the steep streets
mount the sinister cloaks,
leaving flying whirlpools
of scissors in their wake.

At the gate of Bethlehem
the gypsies met.
St Joseph, full of wounds,
wraps a girl in a shroud.
All night long sound
sharp stubborn rifles.

La Virgen cura a los niños
con salivilla de estrella.
Pero la Guardia Civil
avanza sembrando hogueras,
donde joven y desnuda
la imaginación se quema.
Rosa la de los Camborios,
gime sentada en su puerta
con sus dos pechos cortados
puestos en una bandeja.
Y otras muchachas corrían
perseguidas por sus trenzas,
en un aire donde estallan
rosas de pólvora negra.
Cuando todos los tejados
eran surcos en la tierra,
el alba meció sus hombros
en largo perfil de piedra.

*

    ¡Oh ciudad de los gitanos!
La Guardia Civil se aleja
por un túnel de silencio
mientras las llamas te cercan.

    ¡Oh ciudad de los gitanos!
¿Quién te vio y no te recuerda?
Que te busquen en mi frente.
Juego de luna y arena.

The Virgin heals children with
the spittle of stars.
But the Civil Guard
come on, sowing fires,
where, youthful and naked,
imagination burns.
Rosa of the Camborios
moans, sitting on her doorstep,
with her two sliced-off breasts
standing on a tray.
While other girls were running
hair streaming behind them,
through an air where black roses
of powder explode.
When all the roofs
were furrows in the earth,
dawn rocked its shoulders
in a long shape of stone.

*

Oh, city of the gypsies!
The Civil Guard is leaving
through a tunnel of silence
while you are ringed with flame!

Oh, city of the gypsies!
Who that saw you could forget?
On my forehead you'll be found.
Game of moon and game of sand.

Thamar y Amnón

La luna gira en el cielo
sobre las tierras sin agua
mientras el verano siembra
rumores de tigre y llama.
Por encima de los techos
nervios de metal sonaban.
Aire rizado venía
con los balidos de lana.
La tierra se ofrece llena
de heridas cicatrizadas,
o estremecida de agudos
cauterios de luces blancas.

*

Thamar estaba soñando
pájaros en su garganta,
al son de panderos fríos
y cítaras enlunadas.
Su desnudo en el alero,
agudo norte de palma,
pide copos a su vientre
y granizo a sus espaldas.
Thamar estaba cantando
desnuda por la terraza.
Alrededor de sus pies,
cinco palomas heladas.
Amnón, delgado y concreto,
en la torre la miraba,
llenas las ingles de espuma
y oscilaciones la barba.
Su desnudo iluminado
se tendía en la terraza,
con un rumor entre dientes
de flecha recién clavada.
Amnón estaba mirando
la luna redonda y baja,
y vio en la luna los pechos
durísimos de su hermana.

*

Thamar and Amnón

The moon spins in the sky
above lands without water
while the summer sows sounds
of flame and tiger.
Above the roofs ring
metallic nerves.
The frizzled air rises
from bleating herds.
Earth offers itself
full of ancient scars
to the fierce white light
which shakes and sears.

                    *

Thamar was dreaming,
birds in her throat,
cold tambourines,
zithers bathed in moonlight.
On the eaves, her nakedness,
north-star of palm,
pleads for hail and snowflakes
against her skin.
Thamar sang naked
upon the terrace.
Around her feet
four icy pigeons.
Amnón, thin, concrete,
watched from the tower.
His groins full of foam,
his beard shaking for her.
Her luminous nakedness
stretched on the terrace,
between her teeth singing
a freshly-cut arrow.
Amnón was gazing
at the round and low moon
and he saw in the moon
the hard breasts of his sister.

                    *

Amnón a las tres y media
se tendío sobre la cama.
Toda la alcoba sufría
con sus ojos llenos de alas.
La luz, maciza, sepulta
pueblos en la arena parda,
o descubre transitorio
coral de rosas y dalias.
Linfa de pozo oprimida
brota silencio en las jarras.
En el musgo de los troncos
la cobra tendida canta.
Amnón gime por la tela
fresquísima de la cama.
Yedra del escalofrío
cubre su carne quemada.
Thamar entró silenciosa
en la alcoba silenciada,
color de vena y Danubio,
turbia de huellas lejanas.
Thamar, bórrame los ojos
con tu fija madrugada.
Mis hilos de sangre tejen
volantes sobre tu falda.
Déjame tranquila, hermano.
Son tus besos en mi espalda
avispas y vientecillos
en doble enjambre de flautas.
Thamar, en tus pechos altos
hay dos peces que me llaman,
y en las yemas de tus dedos
rumor de rosa encerrada.

                    *

Los cien caballos del rey
en el patio relinchaban.
Sol en cubos resistía
la delgadez de la parra.
Ya la coge del cabello,
ya la camisa le rasga.
Corales tibios dibujan
arroyos en rubio mapa.

                    *

At half past three, Amnón
stretched out on his bed.
With his eyes full of wings
the whole room hurt.
Below the dark sand
the strong light buries villages,
or finds fleeting coral
of roses and dahlias.
Oppressed well-water
sprouts silence in jars.
On the moss of the tree-trunks
the stretched cobra sings.
Between the cold sheets of his bed
Amnón groans.
A shivering, like ivy,
creeps across his parched flesh.
Thamar entered the silenced room
in silence.
Far-off troubles. Colour
of vein and Danube.
'Thamar, blot out my eyes
with your steadfast dawn.
The threads of my blood
weave frills over your skirt.'
'Leave me in peace, brother.
Your kisses are wasps
on my shoulder, light winds
in a dual swarm of flutes.'
'Thamar, in your high breasts
are two fishes that call me,
in the tips of your fingers
a sound of sealed rose.'

                    *

The king's hundred horses
neighed in the patio.
The sun resisted
the slim vine in cubes.
Now he grasps her hair,
now tears her slip.
Warm corals draw streams
on a golden map.

                    *

¡Oh, qué gritos se sentían
por encima de las casas!
Qué espesura de puñales
y túnicas desgarradas.
Por las escaleras tristes
esclavos suben y bajan.
Embolos y muslos juegan
bajo las nubes paradas.
Alrededor de Thamar
gritan vírgenes gitanas
y otras recogen las gotas
de su flor martirizada.
Paños blancos enrojecen
en las alcobas cerradas.
Rumores de tibia aurora
pámpanos y peces cambian.

*

Violador enfurecido,
Amnón huye con su jaca.
Negros le dirigen flechas
en los muros y atalayas.
Y cuando los cuatro cascos
eran cuatro resonancias,
David con unas tijeras
cortó las cuerdas del arpa.

Oh, what shrieks were heard
above the houses!
What thickness of daggers
and ripped-up tunics.
Slaves go up and down
the mournful stairs.
Pistons and thighs work
beneath the still clouds.
Around Thamar, gypsy virgins
scream,
others gather the drops
of her martyrdom.
White sheets turn red
inside locked rooms.
Sounds of a cool dawn
change fishes and vines.

*

Amnón, furious rapist,
flees on his mare.
Negroes aim arrows
from rampart and tower.
And when the four hooves
became four echoes,
David cut the cords of the harp
with scissors.

POET IN NEW YORK

POETA EN NUEVA YORK

1929-1930

POET IN NEW YORK

'New York seems horrible, but for that very reason I'm going there,' wrote Lorca to a friend in June 1929. He had recently suffered an emotional crisis and was extremely depressed when he quit the Old World. He arrived later the same month and stayed until March 1930, when he went for a blissful few weeks to Cuba and had his last sight of New York from the sea in June.

The poet who had sung of Granada's jasmines and pomegranates suddenly found himself thrust into the most modern city on earth. He went to English classes but never learned to speak the language fluently. Nor did he have much contact with fellow-writers in the United States.

What he did do was produce a striking series of poems most of which would remain unpublished in his lifetime. As Richard L. Predmore has noted in *Lorca's New York Poetry*, 'in some ways they read like a book written yesterday. Their themes of materialism, of dehumanisation, of violence, of social and racial injustice could have been taken from today's headlines.'

Like Norman MacCaig in his equally remarkable New York poems, Lorca expresses feelings of culture-shock at the noise, the crowds, the casual violence and the skyscrapers which form, he felt, an inhuman environment. He found the city 'impressive for its coldness and its cruelty. Gold flows there in rivers from all parts of the earth, and death arrives with it.' He was there during the Wall Street crash of October 1929. Ian Gibson describes Lorca writing home that 'for more than seven hours...he had joined the crowd outside the Stock Exchange: it had been a hell of shrieking men and women, exhausted officials slumped to the ground, faintings, the sirens of ambulances and, of course, the suicides, one of which Lorca claimed to have seen with his own eyes, just after the man leapt to his death from a hotel window'. To come to terms with this experience, he needed a new kind of poetic language. While his early work is quite easy to understand, a great deal of *Poet in New York* is baffling, and 'The King of Harlem' and 'Dance of Death', especially, contain passages which are very obscure.

Take the first poem, 'Back from a Walk'. Richard Predmore suggests that the 'shapes' in the first verse are the metropolitan crowds; the serpent is a moving stream of people and traffic and the glass is the innumerable office windows of New York. 'Letting my hair grow' is what everyone does when they die. The trees, children and animals which he sees on his walk through the city

123

lack vitality and perhaps 'the butterfly drowned in the inkwell' is an image of nature destroyed by social organisation.

'Nobody can get a clear idea of what a New York throng is like,' he wrote. '…Well, Walt Whitman, who searched for solitude in it, knew, and T.S. Eliot also knows.' He had read *The Waste Land* in translation and greatly admired it, and perhaps the 'clothed creatures' in '1910' and the 'headless costumes' in 'The King of Harlem' are derived from Eliot's 'hollow men'. But he sympathised deeply with the black Americans and responded to their music and dances.

Of 'The King of Harlem', where that sympathy shines through the often obscure language, he said, 'I wanted to write the poem of the Negro race in North America and emphasise the pain that the blacks suffer in being black in an adverse world; slaves of all the inventions of the white man and of all his machines, with the perpetual fear that they may forget one day to light the gas stove, or steer the automobile, or fasten the starched collar, or stick a fork in their eye. Because the inventions are not theirs.' They were often employed as servants, waiters or cooks, and that is why he writes that simple things like 'dusters, graters, coppers, kitchen saucepans' are beautiful. On the other hand the cars and 'grey metal sheets' of the last verse suggest an industrialism which has run out of control. The references to the 'seller of brandy' and 'those who drink silver whisky' remind us that this was the Prohibition era and that the poor, according to Lorca's letters, were being poisoned by cheap illegal brews. In this poem, crocodiles appear in New York and the primeval forest threatens to make a comeback.

In 'Dance of Death', written after the Wall Street crash, the mysterious mask brings 'sand, alligator, fear' from the jungles of Africa and spells the end of a civilisation based on money. The blacks are not mentioned directly but the mask could be seen as their revenge on white America for uprooting them from their natural environment. In the end Wall Street has gone back to a state of nature and the poet feels it deserves this because of its indifference to human values.

Lorca's growing radicalism extended to the Catholic Church in which he had been brought up. 'Abandoned Church', apparently spoken by a grief-maddened father whose son has been killed in the Great War, suggests that organised religion is no longer relevant. More outspoken is 'Cry to Rome', in which Lorca imagines himself looking back at the Old World from the top of the Chrysler Building, then the tallest in New York. This was written in the wake of the Lateran Treaty between the Church and Mussolini, who is the man urinating on the dove in the first stanza. Christ is still a positive figure but the Pope (the old man in white) talks about love and peace while ignoring the violence around him, and has betrayed Christ's message. The poem ends with a plea for the hungry and oppressed.

There remain the shorter, clearer and perhaps better poems, 'Daybreak' and 'Office and Denunciation', which sum up the total impact of New York on the poet. Dawn in the city is not a time of hope but of unimaginable dreariness. Dirt and noise assault the senses, children are sacrificed to the hunger for money. The great metropolis is built on blood.

The 'Ode to Walt Whitman' was written towards the end of Lorca's time in America, perhaps at sea on the way back from Cuba. By this time, he had got the experience into perspective, and it is a more consistently good poem than the other two long ones. His opening picture of the young men who 'fight with industry' is almost lyrical, but he still stresses that New York is unaware of river, trees and sea (natural life). In the figure of Walt Whitman (1819-92), he contrasts the great American poet and workman's ideals of brotherhood and equality with the corrupt life of 'pansies' in big cities. It is a remarkably frank poem, and while he lived it was published only in a limited edition in Mexico.

'Adam' is included in this sequence, although Lorca himself omitted it, because it was written in New York in December 1929 and because it shares much of its imagery with the 'Ode to Walt Whitman'. There is the Adam-figure, the apple, the 'bloody forest of approaching morning' parallelled by 'morning is wetted by a tree of blood', and the theme of sterility. 'There are bodies not to be repeated in the dawn', the Ode says (does this mean that children are being born only to die?), and the alternative Adam at the end of the sonnet is unable to produce seed.

This section ends, as Lorca intended, with 'Song of the Negroes in Cuba', a hymn of joy as the poet leaves the United States and arrives in a friendlier Spanish-speaking culture.

Vuelta de paseo

Asesinado por el cielo,
entre las formas que van hacia la sierpe
y las formas que buscan el cristal,
dejaré crecer mis cabellos.

Con el árbol de muñones que no canta
y el niño con el blanco rostro de huevo.

Con los animalitos de cabeza rota
y el agua harapienta de los pies secos.

Con todo lo que tiene cansancio sordomudo
y mariposa ahogada en el tintero.

Tropezando con mi rostro distinto de cada día.
¡Asesinado por el cielo!

1910
(Intermedio)

Aquellos ojos míos de mil novecientos diez
no vieron enterrar a los muertos,
ni la feria de ceniza del que llora por la madrugada
ni el corazón que tiembla arrinconado como un caballito de mar.

Aquellos ojos míos de mil novecientos diez
vieron la blanca pared donde orinaban las niñas
el hocico del toro, la seta venenosa
y una luna incomprensible que iluminaba por los rincones
los pedazos de limón seco bajo el negro duro de las botellas.

Aquellos ojos míos en el cuello de la jaca,
en el seno traspasado de Santa Rosa dormida
en los tejados del amor, con gemidos y frescas manos,
en un jardín donde los gatos se comían a las ranas.

Back from a Walk

Assassinated by the sky,
between the shapes that move towards the serpent
and those that move towards the glass,
I'll let my hair grow.

With the tree of amputated limbs, unsinging,
and the child with the blank face of an egg.

With little broken-headed animals
and ragged, dry-footed water.

With all that is exhausted, deaf and dumb
and the butterfly drowned in the inkwell.

Stumbling with my different face each day.
Assassinated by the sky!

1910
(Intermezzo)

Those eyes of mine in 1910
did not see the burial of the dead.
Nor the ashen funfair of the man who wept before dawn,
nor the heart trembling on one side like a sea-horse.

Those eyes of mine in 1910
saw the white wall where the little girls were pissing,
the bull's snout, the poisonous toadstool
and an unknowable moon that lit on the corners
dried lemon scraps beneath the bottles' hard black.

Those eyes of mine saw the neck of the mare,
the pierced bosom of the sleeping Saint Rosa,
on the rooftops of love, with moans and cool hands,
in a garden where cats ate frogs.

Desván donde el polvo viejo congrega estatuas y musgos,
cajas que guardan silencio de cangrejos devorados
en el sitio donde el sueño tropezaba con su realidad.
Allí mis pequeños ojos.

No preguntarme nada. He visto que las cosas
cuando buscan su curso encuentran su vacío.
Hay un dolor de huecos por el aire sin gente
y en mis ojos criaturas vestidas ¡sin desnudo!

[Nueva York, agosto 1929]

El rey de Harlem

Con una cuchara,
arrancaba los ojos a los cocodrilos
y golpeaba el trasero de los monos.
Con una cuchara.

Fuego de siempre dormía en los pedernales
y los escarabajos borrachos de anís
olvidaban el musgo de las aldeas.

Aquel viejo cubierto de setas
iba al sitio donde lloraban los negros
mientras crujía la cuchara del rey
y llegaban los tanques de agua podrida.

Los rosas huían por los filos
de las últimas curvas del aire,
y en los montones de azafrán
los niños machacaban pequeñas ardillas
con un rubor de frenesí manchado.

Es preciso cruzar los puentes
y llegar al rubor negro
para que el perfume de pulmón
nos golpee las sienes con su vestido
de caliente piña.

An attic where old dust piles up on statues and moss.
Chests hold the silence of crabs already eaten.
In the place where the dream stumbles over its reality.
My youthful eyes are there.

Don't ask me anything. I've seen that things
when they seek their way find only their vacuum.
There is an agony of holes in the air without people
and in my eyes clothed creatures – with no bodies!

[New York, August 1929]

The King of Harlem

With a spoon
he scooped out the eyes of crocodiles
and slapped monkeys' bottoms.
With a spoon.

Eternal fire slept in the flints
and beetles drunk on aniseed
forgot the villages' moss.

That old man covered with mushrooms was going
to the place where the negroes wept
meanwhile the king's spoon crackled
and the tanks of stinking water arrived.

The roses fled along the edge
of the last curves of air,
and on the piles of saffron
children squashed little squirrels
with a blush of evil frenzy.

You have to cross the bridges
to find the negro blush
so that the scent of the lung
may beat against our temples
with its dress of warm pineapples.

Es preciso matar al rubio vendedor de aguardiente,
a todos los amigos de la manzana y de la arena,
y es necesario dar con los puños cerrados
a las pequeñas judías que tiemblan llenas de burbujas,
para que el rey de Harlem cante con su muchedumbre,
para que los cocodrilos duerman en largas filas
bajo el amianto de la luna,
y para que nadie dude de la infinita belleza
de los plumeros, los ralladores, los cobres y las cacerolas de las cocinas.

¡Ay Harlem! ¡Ay Harlem! ¡Ay Harlem!
¡No hay angustia comparable a tus rojos oprimidos,
a tu sangre estremecida dentro del eclipse oscuro,
a tu violencia granate sordomuda en la penumbra,
a tu gran rey prisionero con un traje de conserje!

                                    *

Tenía la noche una hendidura y quietas salamandras de marfil.
Las muchachas americanas
llevaban niños y monedas en el vientre,
y los muchachos se desmayaban en la cruz del desperezo.

Ellos son.
Ellos son los que beben el whisky de plata junto a los volcanes
y tragan pedacitos de corazón por las heladas montañas del oso.

Aquella noche el rey de Harlem,
con una durísima cuchara
arrancaba los ojos a los cocodrilos
y golpeaba el trasero de los monos.
Con una cuchara.
Los negros lloraban confundidos
entre paraguas y soles de oro,
los mulatos estiraban gomas, ansiosos de llegar al torso blanco,
y el viento empañaba espejos
y quebraba las venas de los bailarines.

Negros, Negros, Negros, Negros.

La sangre no tiene puertas en vuestra noche boca arriba.
No hay rubor. Sangre furiosa por debajo de las pieles,
viva en la espina del puñal y en el pecho de los paisajes,
bajo las pinzas y las retamas de la celeste luna de cáncer.

You must kill the fair-haired seller of brandy,
and all friends of the apple and the sand,
and you must beat with closed fists
the little French beans which tremble, full of bubbles,
so that the king of Harlem may sing with his multitude,
that crocodiles may sleep in long rows
under the asbestos of the moon,
and that no one may doubt the infinite beauty
of dusters, graters, coppers, kitchen saucepans.

Ah, Harlem, Harlem, Harlem!
There is no anguish to compare with your crushed reds,
your blood shuddering amid a dark eclipse,
your violence – garnet, deaf and dumb in the half-light,
your great king imprisoned in a janitor's uniform.

*

The night cracked open and held quiet salamanders of ivory.
American girls
carried children and coins in their stomachs
and boys fainted on the cross where they were stretched.

They exist.
They are those who drink silver whisky by volcanoes
and who swallow little pieces of heart
upon the icy mountains of the bear.

That night the king of Harlem with a very hard spoon
scooped out the eyes of crocodiles
and slapped monkeys' bottoms.
With a spoon.
The negroes wept bewildered
between umbrellas and golden suns,
mulattos chewed gum, trying to get a white torso,
and the wind clouded mirrors
and broke the dancers' veins.

Negroes, Negroes, Negroes, Negroes.

Blood has no doors in your overturned night.
There is no flush. Furious blood beneath the skin,
living in the thorn of the dagger
and in the heart of landscapes,
under the tweezers and the furze
of the celestial moon of cancer.

Sangre que busca por mil caminos muertes enharinadas y ceniza
     de nardo,
cielos yertos en declive, donde las colonias de planetas
rueden por las playas con los objetos abandonados.

Sangre que mira lenta con el rabo del ojo,
hecha de espartos exprimidos, néctares de subterráneos.
Sangre que oxida el alisio descuidado en una huella
y disuelve a las mariposas en los cristales de la ventana.

Es la sangre que viene, que vendrá
por los tejados y azoteas, por todas partes,
para quemar la clorofila de las mujeres rubias,
para gemir al pie de las camas ante el insomnio de los lavabos
y estrellarse en una aurora de tabaco y bajo amarillo.

Hay que huir,
huir por las esquinas y encerrarse en los últimos pisos,
porque el tuétano del bosque penetrará por las rendijas
para dejar en vuestra carne una leve huella de eclipse
y una falsa tristeza de guante desteñido y rosa química.

Es por el silencio sapientísimo
cuando los camareros y los cocineros y los que limpian con la lengua
las heridas de los millonarios
buscan al rey por las calles o en los ángulos del salitre.

Un viento sur de madera, oblicuo en el negro fango,
escupe a las barcas rotas y se clava puntillas en los hombros;
un viento sur que lleva
colmillos, girasoles, alfabetos
y una pila de Volta con avispas ahogadas.

El olvido estaba expresado por tres gotas de tinta sobre el monóculo;
el amor, por un solo rostro invisible a flor de piedra.
Médulas y corolas componían sobre las nubes
un desierto de tallos sin una sola rosa.

                              *

Blood that seeks, along a thousand routes,
deaths of flour, and ashes of roses,
rigid, slanting skies, where colonies of planets
can roll about the beaches with the flotsam.

Blood that gazes slowly, with the tail of the eye,
made of dried grasses, underground nectar.
Blood rusting the careless trade-wind in a footprint,
and dissolving butterflies against the window.

It is blood that comes, and will come
through the roofs and terraces, from all sides,
to burn the chlorophyll of fair-haired women,
to groan at the foot of beds before the basins' insomnia
to smash against a yellow and tobacco-coloured dawn.

One must flee,
flee round corners, lock oneself on top storeys,
because the marrow of the forest will penetrate through cracks
to leave in your flesh a faint print of eclipse
a false sadness of a discoloured glove and of a chemical rose.

It is in the wisest silence
that waiters and cooks and those who scour with their tongues
the wounds of millionaires
seek the king through streets, on saltpetre corners.

A south wind of wood, slanting through the black mud,
spits at broken boats, drives nails into shoulders;
a south wind that carries
tusks, sunflowers, alphabets
and a battery full of drowned wasps.

Forgetfulness was expressed
by three drops of ink on a monocle,
and love by a single invisible face
on the surface of the stone.
Marrow and corollas formed on the clouds
a desert of stalks, and not one rose.

*

A la izquierda, a la derecha, por el Sur y por el Norte,
se levanta el muro imposible
para el topo y la aguja del agua.
No busquéis, negros, su grieta
para hallar la máscara infinita.
Buscad el gran sol del centro
hechos una piña zumbadora.
El sol que se desliza por los bosques
seguro de no encontrar una ninfa,
el sol que destruye números y no ha cruzado nunca un sueño,
el tatuado sol que baja por el río
y muge seguido de caimanes.

Negros, Negros, Negros, Negros.

Jamás sierpe, ni cebra, ni mula
palidecieron al morir.
El leñador no sabe cuándo expiran
los clamorosos árboles que corta.
Aguardad bajo la sombra vegetal de vuestro rey
a que cicutas y cardos y ortigas turben postreras azoteas.

Entonces, negros, entonces, entonces,
podréis besar con frenesí las ruedas de las bicicletas,
poner parejas de microscopios en las cuevas de las ardillas
y danzar al fin, sin duda, mientras las flores erizadas
asesinan a nuestro Moisés casi en los juncos del cielo.

¡Ay, Harlem disfrazada!
¡Ay, Harlem, amenazada por un gentío de trajes sin cabeza!
Me llega tu rumor,
me llega tu rumor atravesando troncos y ascensores,
a través de láminas grises,
donde flotan tus automóviles cubiertos de dientes,
a través de los caballos muertos y los crímenes diminutos,
a través de tu gran rey desesperado,
cuyas barbas llegan al mar.

To the left, to the right, to south and north,
there rises a wall, impassable
to the mole, the needle of water.
Negroes, do not search for a crevice
to find the infinite mask.
Search for a great central sun
made into a buzzing pineapple.
The sun that slips through the woods
certain not to encounter a nymph,
the sun that destroys numbers and has never crossed a dream,
the tattooed sun that goes down river and bellows
with alligators in pursuit.

Negroes, Negroes, Negroes, Negroes.

Never did snake, zebra or mule
grow pale at death.
The woodcutter does not know
when the noisy trees he cuts, expire.
Wait beneath the vegetable shadow of your king
until hemlocks, thistles and nettles disturb the farthest rooftops.

Then, negroes, then, then,
you can frenziedly kiss bicycle wheels,
put pairs of microscopes in squirrels' nests
and dance at last, no doubt, while the bristling flowers
kill our Moses almost in the reeds of heaven.

Ah, Harlem in disguise!
Ah, Harlem, threatened by a crowd of headless costumes!
Your murmur reaches me,
reaches me through trunks and elevators,
through grey metal sheets,
where your cars are floating, covered with teeth,
through dead horses and petty crimes,
through your great and desperate king
whose beard reaches the sea.

Iglesia abandonada
(Balada de la Gran Guerra)

Yo tenía un hijo que se llamaba Juan.
Yo tenía un hijo.
Se perdió por los arcos un viernes de todos los muertos.
Le vi jugar en las últimas escaleras de la misa
y echaba un cubito de hojalata en el corazón del sacerdote.
He golpeado los ataúdes. ¡Mi hijo! ¡Mi hijo! ¡Mi hijo!
Saqué una pata de gallina por detrás de la luna y luego
comprendí que mi niña era un pez
por donde se alejan las carretas.
Yo tenía una niña.
Yo tenía un pez muerto bajo las cenizas de los incensarios.
Yo tenía un mar. ¿De que? ¡Dios mio! ¡Un mar!
Subí a tocar las campanas, pero las frutas tenían gusanos
y las cerillas apagadas
se comían los trigos de la primavera.
Yo vi la transparente cigüeña de alcohol
mondar las negras cabezas de los soldados agonizantes
y vi las cabañas de goma
donde giraban las copas llenas de lágrimas.
En las anémonas del ofertorio te encontraré, ¡corazón mío!,
cuando el sacerdote levante la mula y el buey con sus fuertes brazos.
para espantar los sapos nocturnos que rondan los helados paisajes
            del cáliz.
Yo tenía un hijo que era un gigante,
pero los muertos son más fuertes y saben devorar pedazos de cielo.
Si mi niño hubiera sido un oso,
yo no temería el sigilo de los caimanes,
ni hubiese visto el mar amarrado a los árboles
para ser fornicado y herido por el tropel de los regimientos.
¡Si mi niño hubiera sido un oso!
Me envolveré sobre esta lona dura para no sentir el frío de los musgos.
Sé muy bien que me darán una manga o la corbata;
pero en el centro de la misa yo romperé el timón y entonces
vendrá a la piedra la locura de pingüinos y gaviotas
que harán decir a los que duermen y a los que cantan por las esquinas:
él tenía un hijo.
¡Un hijo! ¡Un hijo! ¡Un hijo
que no era más que suyo, porque era su hijo!
¡Su hijo! ¡Su hijo! ¡Su hijo!

Abandoned Church
(Ballad of the Great War)

I had a son named John.
I had a son.
He disappeared between the arches on a Friday of death.
I saw him play upon the topmost stairs of the mass
and throw a little tin bucket at the heart of the priest.
I pounded on the coffins. My son! My son! My son!
I pulled a chicken's foot from behind the moon and then,
I understood that my daughter was a fish
through which the carts roll away.
I had a daughter.
I had a dead fish beneath the ash of the censers.
I had a sea. Of what? My God! A sea!
I climbed up to ring the bells, but the fruit was wormy,
the burned-out tapers
were consuming spring wheat.
I saw the transparent stork of alcohol
shave the black heads of dying soldiers
and I saw the rubber huts
where the goblets of tears spin round.
I'll find you, my heart! in the offertory's anemones
when the priest with his vigorous arms raises the mule and the ox
to frighten the night-toads who patrol
the chalice's frozen landscapes.
I had a son who was a giant,
but the dead are stronger, they can eat bits of heaven.
If my son had been a bear,
I would not fear the alligators' cunning,
I wouldn't have seen the sea lashed to the trees
to be raped and mangled by armies.
If my son had been a bear!
I'll wrap myself in this hard canvas not to feel the cold moss.
I know very well that they'll give me a sleeve or the necktie;
but in the centre of the mass I'll break the rudder and then
the madness of penguins and seagulls will come to the stone
and make those who sleep and who sing on the street-corners say:
he had a son.
A son! A son! A son
who was his and his only, because he was his son!
His son! His son! His son!

Danza de la muerte

El mascarón. ¡Mirad el mascarón!
¡Cómo viene del Africa a New York!

Se fueron los árboles de la pimienta,
los pequeños botones de fósforo.
Se fueron los camellos de carne desgarrada
y los valles de luz que el cisne levantaba con el pico.

Era el momento de las cosas secas,
de la espiga en el ojo y el gato laminado,
del óxido de hierro de los grandes puentes
y el definitivo silencio del corcho.

Era la gran reunión de los animales muertos,
traspasados por las espadas de la luz;
la alegría eterna del hipopótamo con las pezuñas de ceniza
y de la gacela con una siempreviva en la garganta.

En la marchita soledad sin onda
el abollado mascarón danzaba.
Medio lado del mundo era de arena,
mercurio y sol dormido el otro medio.

El mascarón. ¡Mirad el mascarón!
¡Arena, caimán y miedo sobre Nueva York!

*

Desfiladeros de cal aprisionaban un cielo vacío
donde sonaban las voces de los que mueren bajo el guano
Un cielo mondado y puro, idéntico a sí mismo,
con el bozo y lirio agudo de sus montañas invisibles,

acabó con los más leves tallitos del canto
y se fue al diluvio empaquetado de la savia,
a través del descanso de los últimos perfiles,
levantando con el rabo pedazos de espejo.

Dance of Death

The mask. Look at the mask!
See it come to New York out of Africa!

The pepper trees went away,
and the little buds of phosphorus.
The camels with torn flesh went away
and the valleys of light that the swan raised on its beak.

It was the time of dry things,
wheat in the eye, and the run-over cat,
the time of rusting iron on great bridges,
and the definitive silence of cork.

It was the great reunion of dead animals,
transfixed by the swords of light;
the eternal delight of the ashen-footed hippo
and the gazelle with a dried flower in her throat.

In the withered solitude, no waves,
the bruised mask danced.
One half of the world was of sand,
the other, sleeping sun and mercury.

The mask. Look at the mask!
Sand, alligator, fear above New York!

*

Lime gorges imprisoned an empty sky,
you heard the voice of those who died beneath the guano.
A sky cleansed and pure, like itself,
with the down and sharp-edged iris of its invisible mountains,

finished with the lightest tendrils of song
and fled to the packed deluge of sap,
across the calm of the last silhouettes,
lifting bits of mirror with its tail.

Cuando el chino lloraba en el tejado
sin encontrar el desnudo de su mujer
y el director del banco observaba el manómetro
que mide el cruel silencio de la moneda,
el mascarón llegaba a Wall Street.

No es extraño para la danza
este columbario que pone los ojos amarillos.
De la esfinge a la caja de caudales hay un hilo tenso
que atraviesa el corazón de todos los niños pobres.
El ímpetu primitivo baila con el ímpetu mecánico,
ignorantes en su frenesí de la luz original.
Porque si la rueda olvida su fórmula,
ya puede cantar desnuda con las manadas de caballos:
y si una llama quema los helados proyectos,
el cielo tendrá que huir ante el tumulto de !as ventanas.

No es extraño este sitio para la danza, yo lo digo.
El mascarón bailará entre columnas de sangre y de números,
entre huracanes de oro y gemidos de obreros parados
que aullarán, noche oscura, por tu tiempo sin luces,
¡oh salvaje Norteamérica!, ¡oh impúdica!, ¡oh salvaje,
tendida en la frontera de la nieve!

El mascarón. ¡Mirad el mascarón!
¡Qué ola de fango y luciérnaga sobre Nueva York!

Yo estaba en la terraza luchando con la luna.
Enjambres de ventanas acribillaban un muslo de la noche.
En mis ojos bebían las dulces vacas de los cielos.
Y las brisas de largos remos
golpeaban los cenicientos cristales de Broadway.

La gota de sangre buscaba la luz de la yema del astro
para fingir una muerta semilla de manzana.
El aire de la llanura, empujado por los pastores,
temblaba con un miedo de molusco sin concha.

Pero no son los muertos los que bailan,
estoy seguro.
Los muertos están embebidos, devorando sus propias manos.

When the Chinaman wept on the roof
without discovering the nakedness of woman,
and the bank director looked at the pressure gauge
that measures the cruel silence of money,
the mask reached Wall Street.

It's not a strange place for the dance,
this columbarium that turns the eyes yellow.
From the sphinx to the treasure-chest goes a taut thread
through the hearts of working-class children.
The primitive impulse and mechanical impulse
dance in frenzy, unaware of the original light.
For if the wheel forgets its formula
it can sing with the horse herds, naked;
and if a flame devours the frozen plans
heaven must flee before the noise of broken windows.

I say, it's not a strange place for the dance.
The mask will dance between columns of blood and of numbers,
between hurricanes of gold and the groans of laid-off workers
who will howl, dark night, for your time without lights.
Oh, savage North America! Shameless and savage!
sprawled on the frontier of snow.

The mask. Look at the mask!
What a wave of filth and glow-worms on New York!

On the terrace I fought with the moon.
Swarms of windows pierced a thigh of the night.
The sweet cows of heaven drank from my eyes.
And the breezes of great oars
hit the ash-coloured glass of Broadway.

The drop of blood sought the light in the yolk of a star
to fake a dead apple seed.
A wind of the plain, pushed by shepherds, quivered
with the fear of a shell-less mollusc.

But the dead do not dance,
I am sure.
The dead are shrunken, gnawing their own fingers.

Son los otros los que bailan con el mascarón y su vihuela;
son los otros, los borrachos de plata, los hombres fríos,
los que crecen en el cruce de los muslos y llamas duras,
los que buscan la lombriz en el paisaje de las escaleras,
los que beben en el banco lágrimas de niña muerta
o los que comen por las esquinas diminutas pirámides del alba.

   ¡Que no baile el Papa!
¡No, que no baile el Papa!
Ni el Rey,
ni el millonario de dientes azules,
ni las bailarinas secas de las catedrales,
ni constructores, ni esmeraldas, ni locos, ni sodomitas.
Solo este mascarón,
este mascarón de vieja escarlatina,
¡solo este mascarón!

   Que ya las cobras silbarán por los últimos pisos,
que ya las ortigas estremecerán patios y terrazas,
que ya la Bolsa será una pirámide de musgo,
que ya vendrán lianas después de los fusiles
y muy pronto, muy pronto, muy pronto.
¡Ay, Wall Street!

   El mascarón. ¡Mirad el mascarón!
¡Cómo escupe veneno de bosque
por la angustia imperfecta de Nueva York!

[Diciembre 1929]

Asesinato
(Des voces de madrugada en Riverside Drive)

¿Cómo fue?
– Una grieta en la mejilla.
¡Eso es todo!
Una uña que aprieta el tallo.
Un alfiler que bucea
hasta encontrar las raicillas del grito.

It's the others who dance, with the mask and with its guitar.
The others, those drunk on silver, the cold men,
those who sleep in the crossing of thighs and hard flames,
who seek the worm in a landscape of stairways,
those who drink in the bank a dead girl's tears
or eat small pyramids of dawn on the corners.

The Pope must not dance!
No, not the Pope!
Nor the King
nor the millionaire with blue teeth
nor the cathedral's fagged dancers,
nor builders, nor emeralds, nor madmen, nor sodomites.
Only this mask,
this mask of old scarlet fever,
only this mask!

Now the cobras will hiss on the topmost floors,
the nettles shake patios and terraces,
the Stock Exchange be turned into a pyramid of moss,
the lianas come after the rifles
and very soon, very soon, very soon now,
Alas, Wall Street!

The mask. Look at the mask!
How it spits the jungle's venom
through New York's imperfect pain!

[December 1929]

Murder
(two voices at dawn on Riverside Drive)

'How did it happen?'
'A gash on the cheek.
That's all!'
A nail which squeezes the stem.
A pin, exploring till it finds
the roots of a scream.

Y el mar deja de moverse.
– *¿Cómo, comó fue?*
– Así.
– *¡Déjame! ¿De esa manera?*
– Sí.
El corazón salió solo.
– *¡Ay, ay de mí!*

La aurora

La aurora de Nueva York tiene
cuatro columnas de cieno
y un huracán de negras palomas
que chapotean las aguas podridas.

La aurora de Nueva York gime
por las inmensas escaleras
buscando entre las aristas
nardos de angustia dibujada.

La aurora llega y nadie la recibe en su boca
porque allí no hay mañana ni esperanza posible.
A veces las monedas en enjambres furiosos
taladran y devoran abandonados niños.

Los primeros que salen comprenden con sus huesos
que no habrá paraíso ni amores deshojados;
saben que van al cieno de números y leyes,
a los juegos sin arte, a sudores sin fruto.

La luz es sepultada por cadenas y ruidos
en impúdico reto de ciencia sin raíces.
Por los barrios hay gentes que vacilan insomnes
como recién salidas de un naufragio de sangre.

And the sea ceases to move.
'How did it happen, how?'
'Like this.'
'Heavens! Like that?'
'Yes.
The heart came out alone'.
'Help, help me!'

Daybreak

The daybreak of New York contains
four columns made of filth
and a hurricane of black doves
that wade in stinking waters.

The daybreak of New York moans
along enormous stairways
and seeks between the ledges
tuberoses, drawn in anguish.

Day breaks, and no one takes it in his mouth
for there no morning is possible, nor hope.
From time to time, a furious shower of coins
perforates and devours abandoned children.

The first to go out understand in their bones
that there will be no heaven or natural love;
they know they are going to a mire of figures,
laws, games without skill, sweat that leads to nothing.

The light is buried by chains and by noises,
challenged shamelessly by rootless science.
Along the suburbs, sleepless crowds are staggering
as though fresh from a shipwreck of blood.

New York

(Oficina y denuncia)

Debajo de las multiplicaciones
hay una gota de sangre de pato.
Debajo de las divisiones
hay una gota de sangre de marinero.
Debajo de las sumas, un río de sangre tierna;
un río que viene cantando
por los dormitorios de los arrabales,
y es plata, cemento o brisa
en el alba mentida de New York.
Existen las montañas, lo sé.
Y los anteojos para la sabiduría,
lo sé. Pero yo no he venido a ver el cielo.
He venido para ver la turbia sangre,
la sangre que lleva las máquinas a las cataratas
y el espíritu a la lengua de la cobra.
Todos los días se matan en New York
cuatro millones de patos,
cinco millones de cerdos,
dos mil palomas para el gusto de los agonizantes,
un millón de vacas,
un millón de corderos
y dos millones de gallos,
que dejan los cielos hechos añicos.
Más vale sollozar afilando la navaja
o asesinar a los perros en las alucinantes cacerías,
que resistir en la madrugada
los interminables trenes de leche,
los interminables trenes de sangre
y los trenes de rosas maniatadas
por los comerciantes de perfumes.
Los patos y las palomas,
y los cerdos y los corderos
ponen sus gotas de sangre
debajo de las multiplicaciones,
y los terribles alaridos de las vacas estrujadas
llenan de dolor el valle
donde el Hudson se emborracha con aceite.

New York
(Office and Denunciation)

Beneath the multiplications
is a drop of duck's blood.
Beneath the divisions
is a drop of the blood of a sailor.
Beneath the statistics, a river of fresh blood;
a river which comes singing
through the bedrooms of the suburbs,
and is silver, cement or breeze
in New York's mendacious dawn.
The mountains exist, I know.
And the eyeglasses for wisdom,
I know. But I have not come to look at the sky.
I have come to see the obscure blood, the blood
that carries the machines to the waterfalls
and the spirit to the tongue of the cobra.
Every day there are killed in New York
four million ducks,
five million pigs,
two thousand doves, to titillate the dying,
one million cows,
one million lambs
and two million cocks
that leave the sky in splinters.
Better to sob as you sharpen the razor
or kill dogs in the dreamlike hunts
than endure in the dawn
the interminable milk trains,
the interminable blood trains,
and the trains of roses, imprisoned
for the merchants of scent.
The ducks and the doves
and the pigs and the lambs
lay their drops of blood
beneath the calculations;
and the terrible outcry of penned-up cattle
fills the valley with pain
where the Hudson runs drunk on oil.

Yo denuncio a toda la gente
que ignora la otra mitad,
la mitad irredimible
que levanta sus montes de cemento
donde laten los corazones
de los animalitos que se olvidan
y donde caeremos todos
en la última fiesta de los taladros.
Os escupo en la cara.
La otra mitad me escucha
devorando, cantando, volando en su pureza,
como los niños de las porterías
que llevan frágiles palitos
a los huecos donde se oxidan
las antenas de los insectos.
No es el infierno, es la calle.
No es la muerte, es la tienda de frutas.
Hay un mundo de ríos quebrados y distancias inasibles
en la patita de ese gato quebrada por el automóvil,
y yo oigo el canto de la lombriz
en el corazón de muchas niñas.
Oxido, fermento, tierra estremecida.
Tierra tú mismo que nadas por los números de la oficina.
¿Qué voy a hacer, ordenar los paisajes?
¿Ordenar los amores que luego son fotografías,
que luego son pedazos de madera y bocanadas de sangre?
No, no; yo denuncio.
Yo denuncio la conjura
de estas desiertas oficinas
que no radian las agonías,
que borran los programas de la selva,
y me ofrezco a ser comido por las vacas estrujadas
quando sus gritos llenan el valle
donde el Hudson se emborracha con aceite.

I denounce all those
who ignore the other half,
the irredeemable half
who raise their mountains of cement
where beat the hearts
of little animals who are forgotten
and where we shall all go down
in the last jamboree of drills.
I spit in your face.
The other half listens to me
eating, urinating, flying in its purity
like the doorkeepers' children
who bear fragile sticks
to the holes where rust
insects' antennae.
This is not hell, but a street.
Not death, but a greengrocer's stall.
Here is a world of tamed rivers and unreachable distances
in that cat's paw smashed by a car,
and I hear the song of the worm
in the hearts of many girl children.
Rust, ferment, shaking of earth.
Earth, you yourself, who float through the office's numbers.
What shall I do? Set the landscapes in order?
Bring order to loves that will shortly be photographs,
that soon will be pieces of wood and mouthfuls of blood?
No, no; I denounce,
I denounce the conspiracy
of these deserted offices
which do not radiate pain,
which blot out the laws of the forest,
and I offer myself to be eaten by those penned-up cattle
when their cries fill the valley
where the Hudson runs drunk on oil.

Grito hacia Roma

(desde la torre del Chrysler Building)

Manzanas levemente heridas
por finos espadines de plata,
nubes rasgadas por una mano de coral
que lleva en el dorso una almendra de fuego,
peces de arsénico como tiburones,
tiburones como gotas de llanto para cegar una multitud,
rosas que hieren
y agujas instaladas en los caños de la sangre,
mundos enemigos y amores cubiertos de gusanos
caerán sobre ti. Caerán sobre la gran cúpula
que unta de aceite las lenguas militares
donde un hombre se orina en una deslumbrante paloma
y escupe carbón machacado
rodeado de miles de campanillas.

Porque ya no hay quien reparta el pan ni el vino,
ni quien cultive hierbas en la boca del muerto,
ni quien abra los linos del reposo,
ni quien llore por las heridas de los elefantes.
No hay más que un millón de herreros
forjando cadenas para los niños que han de venir.
No hay más que un millón de carpinteros
que hacen ataúdes sin cruz.
No hay más que un gentío de lamentos
que se abren las ropas en espera de la bala.
El hombre que desprecia la paloma debía hablar,
debía gritar desnudo entre las columnas,
y ponerse una inyección para adquirir la lepra
y llorar un llanto tan terrible
que disolviera sus anillos y sus teléfonos de diamante.
Pero el hombre vestido de blanco
ignora el misterio de la espiga,
ignora el gemido de la parturienta,
ignora que Cristo puede dar agua todavía,
ignora que la moneda quema el beso de prodigio
y da la sangre del cordero al pico idiota del faisán.

Cry to Rome

(from the Chrysler Building Tower)

Apples lightly scarred
by delicate swords of silver,
clouds torn by a coral fist,
that bears a fiery almond,
arsenic fish like sharks,
sharks like tears, to blind a multitude,
roses which wound
and needles stuck in blood-tubes,
enemy worlds, love covered with worms
will fall on you. Fall on the great dome
that anoints the military tongues with oil
where a man urinates on a radiant dove
and spits a crushed coal, surrounded
by thousands of little bells.

Because now there is no one to share out the bread and wine,
or grow grass in the mouth of the dead,
nor to open the linens of repose,
or weep for the wounded elephants.
Only a million blacksmiths
to forge chains for unborn children.
Only a million carpenters
to make coffins without a cross.
Only a crowd who lament,
undo their clothes, and wait for the bullet.
The man who despises the dove should have spoken,
screamed naked among the columns,
and injected himself with leprosy
and wept with tears so awful
they'd have melted his rings and his diamond telephones.
But the man dressed in white ignores
the mystery of the corn's ear,
ignores the groan of childbirth,
ignores Christ, who can still give water,
ignores the coin that burns the prodigy's kiss
and gives the blood of a lamb
to the pheasant's idiot beak.

Los maestros enseñan a los niños
una luz maravillosa que viene del monte;
pero lo que llega es una reunión de cloacas
donde gritan las oscuras ninfas del cólera.
Los maestros señalan con devoción las enormes cúpulas sahumadas;
pero debajo de las estatuas no hay amor,
no hay amor bajo los ojos de cristal definitivo.
El amor está en las carnes desgarradas por la sed,
en la choza diminuta que lucha con la inundación;
el amor está en los fosos donde luchan las sierpes del hambre,
en el triste mar que mece los cadáveres de las gaviotas
y en el oscurísimo beso punzante debajo de las almohadas.
Pero el viejo de las manos traslúcidas
dirá: amor, amor, amor,
aclamado por millones de moribundos;
dirá: amor, amor, amor,
entre el tisú estremecido de ternura;
dirá: paz, paz, paz,
entre el tirite de cuchillos y melenas de dinamita;
dirá: amor, amor, amor,
hasta que se le pongan de plata los labios.

    Mientras tanto, mientras tanto, ¡ay!, mientras tanto,
los negros que sacan las escupideras,
los muchachos que tiemblan bajo el terror pálido de los directores,
las mujeres ahogadas en aceites minerales,
la muchedumbre de martillo, de violín o de nube,
ha de gritar aunque le estrellen los sesos en el muro,
ha de gritar frente a las cúpulas,
ha de gritar loca de fuego,
ha de gritar loca de nieve,
ha de gritar con la cabeza llena de excremento,
ha de gritar como todas las noches juntas,
ha de gritar con voz tan desgarrada
hasta que las ciudades tiemblen como niñas
y rompan las prisiones del aceite y la música,
porque queremos el pan nuestro de cada día,
flor de aliso y perenne ternura desgranada,
porque queremos que se cumpla la voluntad de la Tierra
que da sus frutos para todos.

The masters show the children
a wonderful light coming from the mountain;
but what comes is a meeting-place of sewers
where the dark nymphs of cholera scream.
The masters point with devotion to great fumigated domes;
but there is no love beneath the statues,
no love beneath the eyes of fixed crystal.
Love is in the flesh racked by thirst,
in the hovel that resists the flood;
in the ditches where the serpents of hunger make war,
in the sad sea that rocks the gulls' corpses
and in the darkest kiss that stings beneath the pillows.
But the old man with translucent hands
will say: Love, love, love,
cheered by millions of the dying;
will say: love, love, love,
in the shuddering tissue of tenderness;
will say: peace, peace, peace,
among the shivering knives and dynamite melons;
will say: love, love, love,
until his lips turn silver.

Meanwhile, meanwhile, ah! meanwhile,
the negroes who take out the spitoons,
the boys who tremble under the directors' pale terror,
women drowned in mineral oil,
the crowd of hammer, violin or cloud,
must cry out though they shatter their brains on a wall,
cry out in front of the domes,
cry out maddened by fire,
and by snow,
cry out with a head full of excrement,
cry like all nights made one,
cry with a voice so torn
that the cities will tremble like girls
and break the prisons of oil and of music,
because we want our daily bread,
the alder flower, threshed tenderness perennial,
because we want to accomplish the will of the Earth
that gives her fruits to all.

Oda a Walt Whitman

Por el East River y el Bronx
los muchachos cantaban enseñando sus cinturas,
con la rueda, el aceite, el cuero y el martillo.
Noventa mil mineros sacaban la plata de las rocas
y los niños dibujaban escaleras y perspectivas.

Pero ninguno se dormía,
ninguno quería ser el río,
ninguno amaba las hojas grandes,
ninguno la lengua azul de la playa.

Por el East River y el Queensborough
los muchachos luchaban con la industria,
y los judíos vendían al fauno del río
la rosa de la circuncisión
y el cielo desembocaba por los puentes y los tejados
manadas de bisontes empujadas por el viento.

Pero ninguno se detenía,
ninguno quería ser nube,
ninguno buscaba los helechos
ni la rueda amarilla del tamboril.

Cuando la luna salga
las poleas rodarán para turbar el cielo;
un límite de agujas cercará la memoria
y los ataúdes se llevarán a los que no trabajan.

Nueva York de cieno,
Nueva York de alambre y de muerte.
¿Qué ángel llevas oculto en la mejilla?
¿Qué voz perfecta dirá las verdades del trigo?
¿Quién el sueño terrible de tus anémonas manchadas?

Ni un solo momento, viejo hermoso Walt Whitman,
he dejado de ver tu barba llena de mariposas,
ni tus hombros de pana gastados por la luna,
ni tus muslos de Apolo virginal,
ni tu voz como una columna de ceniza;

Ode to Walt Whitman

Along East River and the Bronx
bare-chested youths were singing,
with the wheel, the oil, the leather and the hammer.
Ninety thousand miners dug silver from the rocks
and little boys designed stairs and perspectives.

But none would sleep,
none wanted to be a river,
none liked the great leaves
or the beach's blue tongue.

In East River and in Queensborough
the young men fought with industry,
and the Jews sold the faun of the river
the rose of circumcision
and the sky through bridges and roofs
poured herds of bison driven by the wind.

But none would pause,
none wanted to be a cloud,
none looked for ferns
or the tambourine's yellow wheel.

When the moon rises
pulleys turn and pull down the sky;
a ring of needles will imprison your memory
and those who don't work will be brought out in coffins.

New York of slime,
New York of wires and death.
What angel do you hide in your cheek?
What perfect voice will speak the truths of the wheat?
Or your terrible dream of soiled anemones?

Not for one moment – aged, beautiful Walt Whitman –
have I failed to see your beard full of butterflies,
nor your corduroy shoulders, wasted by the moon,
nor your thighs of virginal Apollo,
nor your voice like a pillar of ash;

anciano hermoso como la niebla
que gemías igual que un pájaro
con el sexo atravesado por una aguja,
enemigo del sátiro,
enemigo de la vid
y amante de los cuerpos bajo la burda tela.
Ni un solo momento, hermosura viril
que en montes de carbón, anuncios y ferrocarriles,
soñabas ser un río y dormir como un río
con aquel camarada que pondría en tu pecho
un pequeño dolor de ignorante leopardo.

Ni un solo momento, Adán de sangre, macho,
hombre solo en el mar, viejo hermoso Walt Whitman,
porque por las azoteas,
agrupados en los bares,
saliendo en racimos de las alcantarillas,
temblando entre las piernas de los chauffeurs
o girando en las plataformas del ajenjo,
los maricas, Walt Whitman, te señalan.

¡También ese! ¡También! Y se despeñan
sobre tu barba luminosa y casta,
rubios del norte, negros de la arena,
muchedumbres de gritos y ademanes,
como gatos y como las serpientes,
los maricas, Walt Whitman, los maricas
turbios de lágrimas, carne para fusta,
bota o mordisco de los domadores.

¡También ese! ¡También! Dedos teñidos
apuntan a la orilla de tu sueño
cuando el amigo come tu manzana
con un leve sabor de gasolina
y el sol canta por los ombligos
de los muchachos que juegan bajo los puentes.

Pero tú no buscabas los ojos arañados,
ni el pantano oscurísimo donde sumergen a los niños,
ni la saliva helada,
ni las curvas heridas como panza de sapo
que llevan los maricas en coches y terrazas
mientras la luna los azota por las esquinas del terror.

old man, beautiful as the mist,
how you moaned like a bird
with its sex transfixed by a needle,
enemy of satyrs,
enemy of vines,
and lover of bodies under rough cloth.
Not for one moment, virile beauty,
who in mountains of coal, billboards and railways,
dreamed of being a river, and sleeping like a river
with that comrade who would lay in your breast
the small pain of an ignorant leopard.

Not for one moment, Adam of blood, male,   ·
lone man in the sea, aged, beautiful Walt Whitman,
because in the terraces,
crowded in bars,
coming in bunches out of sewers,
trembling between chauffeurs' legs,
or whirling on the platforms of absinth,
the pansies, Walt Whitman, point to you.

That one also! Also! And they hurl themselves
on your chaste and luminous beard,
fair-haired northerners, negroes from the sand,
multitudes who bawl and gesticulate
like cats and like serpents,
the pansies, Walt Whitman, the pansies,
swollen with tears, flesh for the whip,
the boot or bite of the masters.

That one also! Also! Dirty fingers
point to the edge of your dream
while a friend eats your apple
with its faint taste of petrol
and the sun sings around the navels
of boys playing under the bridge.

But you were not looking for the scratched eyes,
nor the dark swamp where children drown,
nor the frozen saliva,
nor the curved wounds like the paunch of a toad
which the pansies carry in cars and in terraces –
the moon whips them around corners of fear.

Tú buscabas un desnudo que fuera como un río,
toro y sueño que junte la rueda con el alga,
padre de tu agonía, camelia de tu muerte,
y gimiera en las llamas de tu ecuador oculto.

Porque es justo que el hombre no busque su deleite
en la selva de sangre de la mañana próxima.
El cielo tiene playas donde evitar la vida
y hay cuerpos que no deben repetirse en la aurora.

Agonía, agonía, sueño, fermento y sueño.
Este es el mundo, amigo, agonía, agonía.
Los muertos se descomponen bajo el reloj de las ciudades,
la guerra pasa llorando con un millón de ratas grises,
los ricos dan a sus queridas
pequeños moribundos iluminados,
y la vida no es noble, ni buena, ni sagrada.

Puede el hombre, si quiere, conducir su deseo
por vena de coral o celeste desnudo.
Mañana los amores serán rocas y el Tiempo
una brisa que viene dormida por las ramas.

Por eso no levanto mi voz, viejo Walt Whitman,
contra el niño que escribe
nombre de niña en su almohada,
ni contra el muchacho que se viste de novia
en la oscuridad del ropero,
ni contra los solitarios de los casinos
que beben con asco el agua de la prostitución
ni contra los hombres de mirada verde
que aman al hombre y queman sus labios en silencio.
Pero sí contra vosotros, maricas de las ciudades,
de carne tumefacta y pensamiento inmundo,
madres de lodo, arpías, enemigos sin sueño
del Amor que reparte coronas de alegría.

Contra vosotros siempre, que dais a los muchachos
gotas de sucia muerte con amargo veneno.
Contra vosotros siempre,
Faeries de Norteamérica,
Pájaros de la Habana,

You sought a nakedness like a river,
a bull, a dream that joins the seaweed to the wheel,
father of your agony, camelia of your death,
moans in the blaze of your hidden equator.

Because it is just that man seeks not his delight
in the bloody forest of approaching morning.
Heaven has shores where life can be avoided,
there are bodies not to be repeated in the dawn.

Agony, agony, dream, ferment, dream.
Such is the world, my friend, agony.
The dead decompose below city clocks,
war passes with a million grey rats weeping,
the rich give their lady friends
tiny lit-up dying things,
and life is not noble, good or holy.

Man can, if he wishes, channel his desire
through a coral vein or a celestial nude.
Tomorrow, love affairs will be rocks, and Time
a breeze that comes, asleep, through the branches.

That is why I do not raise my voice, aged Walt Whitman,
against the little boy who writes
the name of a girl on his pillow,
nor against the youth who clothes himself as a bride
in the darkness of the wardrobe,
nor against the lonely men in casinos
who drink with loathing prostitution's water,
nor against the men of green glance
who love men and burn their lips in silence.
But yes, against you, pansies of the cities,
of swollen flesh and unclean thought,
dregs of mud, harpies, sleepless enemies
of the Love which gives crowns of delight.

Against you always, you who give the young
drops of filthy death with bitter poison.
Against you always,
Fairies of North America,
Pájaros of Havana,

Jotos de Méjico,
Sarasas de Cádiz,
Apios de Sevilla,
Cancos de Madrid,
Floras de Alicante,
Adelaidas de Portugal.

¡Maricas de todo el mundo, asesinos de palomas!
Esclavos de la mujer, perras de sus tocadores,
abiertos en las plazas con fiebre de abanico
o emboscados en yertos paisajes de cicuta.

¡No haya cuartel! La muerte
mana de vuestros ojos
y agrupa flores grises en la orilla del cieno.
¡No haya cuartel! ¡Alerta!
Que los confundidos, los puros,
los clásicos, los señalados, los suplicantes
os cierren las puertas de la bacanal.

Y tú, bello Walt Whitman, duerme a orillas del Hudson
con la barba hacia el polo y las manos abiertas.
Arcilla blanda o nieve, tu lengua está llamando
camaradas que velen tu gacela sin cuerpo.
Duerme, no queda nada.
Una danza de muros agita las praderas
y América se anega de máquinas y llanto.
Quiero que el aire fuerte de la noche más honda
quite flores y letras del arco donde duermes
y un niño negro anuncie a los blancos del oro
la llegada del reino de la espiga.

Jotos of Mexico,
Sarasas of Cadiz,
Apios of Seville,
Cancos of Madrid,
Floras of Alicante,
Adelaidas of Portugal.

Pansies of the whole world, killers of doves!
Slaves of women, bitches of their boudoirs,
open in the squares with the fever of a fan
or ambushed in stark landscapes of hemlock.

Let there be no quarter! Death
flows from your eyes
and heaps grey flowers on the muddy shore.
Let there be no quarter! Look out!
Let the bewildered, the pure,
the classical, the famous, the supplicants,
close on you the bacchanalian gates.

And you, beautiful Walt Whitman, sleep on Hudson's banks,
your beard towards the pole, your hands open.
Soft clay or snow, your tongue is calling
on comrades to watch your dream-gazelle.
Sleep, for nothing remains.
A dancing of walls disturbs the prairies
and America is flooded with machines and with tears.
I want the strong wind of profoundest night
to take flowers, to take writing from the arch where you sleep,
and a black child to announce to the money-grubbing whites
the reign of the ear of corn.

F

Adán

Arbol de sangre moja la mañana
por donde gime la recién parida.
Su voz deja cristales en la herida
y un gráfico de hueso en la ventana.

  Mientras la luz que viene fija y gana
blancas metas de fábula que olvida
el tumulto de venas en la huida
hacia el turbio frescor de la manzana.

  Adán sueña en la fiebre de la arcilla
un niño que se acerca galopando
por el doble latir de su mejilla.

  Pero otro Adán oscuro está soñando
neutra luna de piedra sin semilla
donde el niño de luz se irá quemando.

Adam

Morning is wetted by a tree of blood
where the newly delivered woman groans.
Her voice leaves glass within the wound
and in the window a diagram of bones.

Meanwhile the steadily advancing light
meets the white boundaries of a fable,
forgetting the tumult of the veins, in flight
towards the troubled coolness of the apple.

Adam dreams in the fever of the clay
a child who comes towards him, galloping
through the double throbbing of his cheek.

But another dark Adam is dreaming
a neutral stony moon without a seed
in which that child of light will burn one day.

Son de negros en Cuba

Cuando llegue la luna llena
iré a Santiago de Cuba.
Iré a Santiago.
En un coche de agua negra.
Iré a Santiago.
Cantarán los techos de palmera.
Iré a Santiago.
Cuando la palma quiere ser cigüeña.
Iré a Santiago.
Y cuando quiere ser medusa el plátano.
Iré a Santiago.
Con la rubia cabeza de Fonseca.
Iré a Santiago.
Y con el rosa de Romeo y Julieta.
Iré a Santiago.
Mar de papel y plata de monedas.
Iré a Santiago.
¡Oh Cuba, oh ritmo de semillas secas!
Iré a Santiago.
¡Oh cintura caliente y gota de madera!
Iré a Santiago.
¡Arpa de troncos vivos, caimán, flor de tabaco!
Iré a Santiago.
Siempre dije que yo iría a Santiago
en un coche de agua negra.
Iré a Santiago.
Brisa y alcohol en las ruedas.
Iré a Santiago.
Mi coral en la tiniebla.
Iré a Santiago.
El mar ahogado en la arena.
Iré a Santiago.
Calor blanco, fruta muerta.
Iré a Santiago.
¡Oh bovino frescor de cañavera!
¡Oh Cuba! ¡Oh curva de suspiro y barro!
Iré a Santiago.

[La Habana, abril 1930]

Song of the Negroes in Cuba

When the full moon comes up, I'll go to Santiago, Cuba,
I'll go to Santiago
in a coach of black water.
I'll go to Santiago.
The roofs of palm will sing.
I'll go to Santiago.
When the palm tree wants to be a stork,
I'll go to Santiago.
And when the banana tree wants to be a jellyfish,
I'll go to Santiago.
I'll go to Santiago
with the fair head of Fonseca.
I'll go to Santiago.
With Romeo and Juliet's rose
I'll go to Santiago.
Sea of paper, silver coins.
I'll go to Santiago.
Oh, Cuba! Oh rhythm of dried seeds!
I'll go to Santiago.
Oh, warm waist and drop of wood!
I'll go to Santiago.
Harp of living trunks. Crocodile. Tobacco flower.
I'll go to Santiago.
I always said I'd go to Santiago
in a coach of black water.
I'll go to Santiago.
Breeze and liquor on the wheels,
I'll go to Santiago.
My coral in the darkness,
I'll go to Santiago.
The sea smothered in the sand,
I'll go to Santiago.
White heat and dead fruit,
I'll go to Santiago.
Oh, cowlike freshness of the sugar-cane!
Oh, Cuba! Oh, curve of sighs and clay!
I'll go to Santiago.

[Havana, April 1930]

DIVÁN DEL TAMARIT

DIVÁN DEL TAMARIT

1936

DIVÁN DEL TAMARIT

These poems were written in the early 1930s, after Lorca's return from America, and formed part of a book never published in his lifetime. It was intended to be a tribute to the old Arab poets of Granada whom he had read in translation. *Diván* means collection, *tamarit* means literally 'abundant in dates' and was the name of his uncle's estate. The *gacela* and *casida* were Arab poetic forms – usually erotic.

The Arabs had vanished long ago, although the poet had grown up among traces of their culture. In 1492 Granada fell to the 'Catholic kings', Ferdinand and Isabella, clearing the way for the Inquisition and the expulsion of Jews and Moors from Spain. Lorca said of this only two months before his death:

> It was a disastrous event, even though they may say the opposite in the schools. An admirable civilisation, and a poetry, architecture and sensitivity unique in the world – all were lost, to give way to an impoverished, cowed city...where the worst middle class in Spain today is busy stirring things up.

This 'worst middle class in Spain' would be mortally offended by his views.

So perhaps it is significant that Lorca associated himself with pagan love songs rather than Catholic hymns. But these are not hedonistic, Omar Kháyyám-like poems; they are desperately sad. Lorca is more conscious than ever of his mortality, of the hard landscape of bone beneath the skin, and of how he personally can transcend death only by writing poetry – 'all should know that I have not died', as he says in an almost prophetic passage in the 'Gacela of the Dark Death'.

Prophetic, too, is the line 'Blood will resound through little rooms', in the 'Casida of the Reclining Woman' who perhaps can be identified with the earth. It was as if, with his poet's instinct, he sensed the violence to come.

Gacela del amor imprevisto

Nadie comprendía el perfume
de la oscura magnolia de tu vientre.
Nadie sabía que martirizabas
un colibrí de amor entre los dientes.

Mil caballitos persas se dormían
en la plaza con luna de tu frente,
mientras que yo enlazaba cuatro noches
tu cintura, enemiga de la nieve.

Entre yeso y jazmines, tu mirada
era un pálido ramo de simientes.
Yo busqué, para darte, por mi pecho
las letras de marfil que dicen *siempre*,

siempre, siempre: jardín de mi agonía,
tu cuerpo fugitivo para siempre,
la sangre de tus venas en mi boca,
tu boca ya sin luz para mi muerte.

Gacela de la terrible presencia

Yo quiero que el agua se quede sin cauce.
Yo quiero que el viento se quede sin valles.

Quiero que la noche se quede sin ojos
y mi corazón sin la flor del oro;

que los bueyes hablen con las grandes hojas
y que la lombriz se muera de sombra;

que brillen los dientes de la calavera
y los amarillos inunden la seda.

Puedo ver el duelo de la noche herida
luchando enroscada con el mediodía.

Gacela of Unforeseen Love

Nobody understood the perfume
of the dark magnolia of your womb.
Nobody knew that you crushed to death
a humming-bird of love between your teeth.

A thousand little Persian horses slumbered
in the moonlit plaza of your forehead,
meanwhile through four nights I embraced
the enemy of snow, your waist.

Between the plaster and the jasmines, your glance
was a pale, seed-bearing branch.
I sought to give you, in my breast,
the ivory letters that spell *always*,

always, always: garden of my agony,
your body always fleeing from me,
the blood of your veins in my mouth,
and yours already lightless for my death.

Gacela of the Terrible Presence

I want the water to lose its course.
The wind to lose its valleys.

I want the night to lose its eyes
and my heart its golden flower;

that the oxen should speak with great leaves
and the earthworm perish in darkness;

that the teeth of the skull should glisten
and yellows flood the silk.

I can see the duel of the wounded night
that wrestles with midday.

Resisto un ocaso de verde veneno
y los arcos rotos donde sufre el tiempo.

Pero no ilumines tu limpio desnudo
como un negro cactus abierto en los juncos.

Déjame en un ansia de oscuros planetas,
pero no me enseñes tu cintura fresca.

Gacela del amor desesperado

La noche no quiere venir
para que tú no vengas,
ni yo pueda ir.

Pero yo iré,
aunque un sol de alacranes me coma la sien.

Pero tú vendrás
con la lengua quemada por la lluvia de sal.

El día no quiere venir
para que tú no vengas,
ni yo pueda ir.

Pero yo iré
entregando a los sapos mi mordido clavel.

Pero tú vendrás
por las turbias cloacas de la oscuridad.

Ni la noche ni el día quieren venir
para que por ti muera
y tú mueras por mí.

I resist a green poisonous sunset
and broken arches where time is suffering.

But do not lighten your clear nakedness
like a black cactus open in the reeds.

Leave me in a fever of dark planets
but do not show me your cool waist.

Gacela of Desperate Love

The night doesn't want to come,
so you cannot come
and I cannot go.

But I will go
although a scorpion sun may eat my temples.

But you will come
with your tongue burned by the salt rain.

The day doesn't want to come
so you cannot come
and I cannot go.

But I will go,
leaving the toads my chewed carnation.

But you will come
through the muddy sewers of dark.

Neither night nor day want to come
so I may die for you
and you for me.

Gacela del niño muerto

Todas las tardes en Granada,
todas las tardes se muere un niño.
Todas las tardes el agua se sienta
a conversar con sus amigos.

    Los muertos llevan alas de musgo.
El viento nublado y el viento limpio
son dos faisanes que vuelan por las torres
y el día es un muchacho herido.

    No quedaba en el aire ni una brizna de alondra
cuando yo te encontré por las grutas del vino.
No quedaba en la tierra ni una miga de nube
cuando te ahogabas por el río.

    Un gigante de agua cayó sobre los montes
y el valle fue rodando con perros y con lirios.
Tu cuerpo, con la sombra violeta de mis manos,
era, muerto en la orilla, un arcángel de frío.

Gacela de la muerte oscura

Quiero dormir el sueño de las manzanas,
alejarme del tumulto de los cementerios.
Quiero dormir el sueño de aquel niño
que quería cortarse el corazón en alta mar.

    No quiero que me repitan que los muertos no pierden la sangre;
que la boca podrida sigue pidiendo agua.
No quiero enterarme de los martirios que da la hierba,
ni de la luna con boca de serpiente
que trabaja antes del amanecer.

    Quiero dormir un rato,
un rato, un minuto, un siglo;
pero que todos sepan que no he muerto;

Gacela of the Dead Child

Each afternoon in Granada,
each afternoon a child dies.
Each afternoon the water sits down
to chat among its friends.

The dead wear wings of moss.
The winds are clear and cloudy,
they are two pheasants that fly through the towers
and the day is a wounded boy.

Not a fragment of lark was left in the sky
when I met you in caverns of wine.
Not a crumb of cloud was left on earth
when you were drowned in the river.

A giant of water fell over the hills,
dogs and lilies rolled round the valley.
Through the violet shadow of my hands, your corpse
on the bank, was a cold archangel.

Gacela of the Dark Death

I want to sleep the sleep of apples,
to leave behind the noise of cemeteries.
I want to sleep as did that child who wanted
to cut his heart on the high seas.

I do not want to hear again that corpses keep their blood,
nor of the thirst the rotting mouth can't slake.
I do not want to know of the torments grass gives,
nor of the moon with a snake's mouth
that toils before daybreak.

I want to sleep for a short time,
a short time, a minute, a hundred years;
but all should know that I have not died,

que hay un establo de oro en mis labios;
que soy el pequeño amigo del viento Oeste;
que soy la sombra inmensa de mis lágrimas.

Cúbreme por la aurora con un velo,
porque me arrojará puñados de hormigas,
y moja con agua dura mis zapatos
para que resbale la pinza de su alacrán.

Porque quiero dormir el sueño de las manzanas
para aprender un llanto que me limpie de tierra;
porque quiero vivir con aquel niño oscuro
que quería cortarse el corazón en alta mar.

Gacela de la huida

Me he perdido muchas veces por el mar
con el oído lleno de flores recién cortadas,
con la lengua llena de amor y de agonía.
Muchas veces me he perdido por el mar,
como me pierdo en el corazón de algunos niños.

No hay noche que, al dar un beso,
no sienta la sonrisa de las gentes sin rostro,
ni hay nadie que, al tocar un recién nacido,
olvide las inmóviles calaveras de caballo.

Porque las rosas buscan en la frente
un duro paisaje de hueso
y las manos del hombre no tienen más sentido
que imitar a las raíces bajo tierra.

Como me pierdo en el corazón de algunos niños,
me he perdido muchas veces por el mar.
Ignorante del agua voy buscando
una muerte de luz que me consuma.

that there is a stable of gold on my lips,
that I am the friend of the west wind,
that I am the vast shadow of my tears.

Cover me with a veil,
throw fistfuls of ants at me at dawn,
and wet my shoes with hard water,
that it may slide on pincers like a scorpion.

Because I want to sleep the sleep of apples,
to learn a lament that will purify me;
because I want to stay with that dark child who wanted
to cut his heart on the high seas.

Gacela of the Flight

Many times I have lost myself in the sea
with my ears full of freshly cut flowers
and with my tongue full of love and pain.
Many times I have lost myself in the sea
as I do in the heart of certain children.

There is no night when, in giving a kiss,
I do not feel the smile of faceless people,
and no one who, in touching a newborn child,
forgets the horse's motionless skull.

Because roses search in the forehead
for a hard landscape of bone,
and the hands of man have no other object
than to imitate the roots below the earth.

As I lose myself in the heart of certain children
many times I have been lost in the sea.
Unaware of the water, I search for death
and the light of that death consumes me.

Casida del herido por el agua

Quiero bajar al pozo,
quiero subir los muros de Granada,
para mirar el corazón pasado
por el punzón oscuro de las aguas.

El niño herido gemía
con una corona de escarcha.
Estanques, aljibes y fuentes
levantaban al aire sus espadas.
¡Ay qué furia de amor, qué hiriente filo,
qué nocturno rumor, qué muerte blanca!
¡Qué desiertos de luz iban hundiendo
los arenales de la madrugada!
El niño estaba solo
con la ciudad dormida en la garganta.
Un surtidor que viene de los sueños
lo defiende del hambre de las algas.
El niño y su agonía frente a frente,
eran dos verdes lluvias enlazadas.
El niño se tendía por la tierra
y su agonía se curvaba.

Quiero bajar al pozo,
quiero morir mi muerte a bocanadas,
quiero llenar mi corazón de musgo,
para ver al herido por el agua.

Casida del llanto

He cerrado mi balcón
porque no quiero oír el llanto,
pero por detrás de los grises muros
no se oye otra cosa que el llanto.

Hay muy pocos ángeles que canten,
hay muy pocos perros que ladren,
mil violines caben en la palma de mi mano.

Casida of One Wounded by the Water

I want to go down to the well, I want
to climb the walls of Granada,
to see the heart that has been pierced
by the dark needle of water.

The wounded boy was groaning
his head crowned with white frost.
Ponds, cisterns and fountains
raised to the air their swords.
Ah, what fury of love, what a cutting edge,
dark murmurs, a death so white!
Sunk in the sands of daybreak,
what deserts of light!
The boy was alone, the city
in his throat, asleep.
A spout of dreams protects him from
the hunger of seaweed.
The boy and his agony, face to face,
were two green rains entwined.
The boy stretched out upon the earth,
his agony curved round.

I want to go down to the well, I want
to die my death by mouthfuls,
to fill my heart with moss, to see
one wounded by the water.

Casida of the Weeping

I have shut my balcony window.
I don't want to hear the weeping.
Yet, behind the grey walls, nothing
is heard except the weeping.

There are very few angels that sing,
there are very few dogs that bark.
A thousand violins fit into the palm of my hand.

Pero el llanto es un perro inmenso,
el llanto es un ángel inmenso,
el llanto es un violín inmenso,
las lágrimas amordazan al viento,
y no se oye otra cosa que el llanto.

Casida de la mujer tendida

Verte desnuda es recordar la tierra.
La tierra lisa, limpia de caballos.
La tierra sin un junco, forma pura
cerrada al porvenir: confín de plata.

Verte desnuda es comprender el ansia
de la lluvia que busca débil talle,
o la fiebre del mar de inmenso rostro
sin encontrar la luz de su mejilla.

La sangre sonará por las alcobas
y vendrá con espada fulgurante,
pero tú no sabrás dónde se ocultan
el corazón de sapo o la violeta.

Tu vientre es una lucha de raíces,
tus labios son un alba sin contorno,
bajo las rosas tibias de la cama
los muertos gimen esperando turno.

Casida de la rosa

La rosa
no buscaba la aurora:
casi eterna en su ramo,
buscaba otra cosa.

But the weeping is a great dog,
the weeping is a great angel,
and an immense violin.
Tears are gagging the wind
and nothing is heard but the weeping.

Casida of the Reclining Woman

To see you naked is to remember the earth.
The flat earth, emptied of horses.
The earth without a rush, pure shape
closed to the future: a silver boundary.

To see you naked is to understand the desire
of the rain that seeks a fragile form,
or the fever of the sea's great face
which can't find the light of its cheek.

Blood will resound through little rooms
and will come with swords flaming,
but you will not know where they conceal themselves,
the toad's heart, the violet.

Your stomach is a struggling of roots,
your lips are a formless daybreak.
Under the lukewarm roses of your bed
the dead moan, waiting their turn.

Casida of the Rose

The rose
was not looking for the daybreak:
almost eternal on its branch
it looked for something else.

La rosa
no buscaba ni ciencia ni sombra:
confín de carne y sueño,
buscaba otra cosa.

La rosa
no buscaba la rosa.
Inmóvil por el cielo,
buscaba otra cosa.

Casida de las palomas oscuras

Por las ramas del laurel
vi dos palomas oscuras.
La una era el sol,
la otra la luna.
«Vecinitas», les dije,
«¿dónde está mi sepultura?»
«En mi cola», dijo el sol.
«En mi garganta», dijo la luna.
Y yo que estaba caminando
con la tierra por la cintura
vi dos águilas de nieve
y una muchacha desnuda.
La una era la otra
y la muchacha era ninguna.
«Aguilitas», les dije,
«¿dónde está mi sepultura?»
«En mi cola», dijo el sol.
«En mi garganta», dijo la luna.
Por las ramas del laurel
vi dos palomas desnudas.
La una era la otra
y las dos eran ninguna.

The rose
was not looking for knowledge, or for shadow:
the boundary of flesh and dream
it looked for something else.

The rose
was not looking for the rose.
Unmoving in the sky
it looked for something else.

Casida of the Dark Doves

I saw two dark doves
through the branches of laurel.
The one was the sun,
and the other the moon.
'Little neighbours,' I said to them,
'where is my tomb?'
'In my tail,' said the sun.
'In my throat,' said the moon.
And I who was walking
with the globe at my belt
saw two snowy eagles
and a girl, who was naked.
The one was the other,
and the girl was no one.
'Little eagles,' I said to them,
'where is my tomb?'
'In my tail,' said the sun.
'In my throat,' said the moon.
I saw two naked doves
through the branches of laurel.
The one was the other
and the two were no one.

LAMENT FOR
IGNACIO SÁNCHEZ MEJÍAS
LLANTO POR IGNACIO SÁNCHEZ MEJÍAS

1935

LAMENT FOR IGNACIO SÁNCHEZ MEJÍAS

Ignacio Sánchez Mejías, born in 1891, was a brave and very famous bullfighter, but not a typical one. He retired more than once to devote himself to flamenco and literature, he had written a play and was friendly with several poets, and Lorca had known him for years.

When Ignacio returned to the ring for the last time he was over forty and it seemed a reckless thing to do. He was attacked by a bull at Manzanares on 11 August 1934. 'Ignacio tried to get to his feet but the animal turned suddenly and sank a horn deep into his thigh, tossed him to the ground and gored him furiously. When they managed to get the bull away, Sánchez Mejías was lying in a pool of blood, and, as he was carried to the infirmary, he left a thick red trail across the sand' (Ian Gibson). He developed gangrene and died two days later in Madrid after much suffering. Lorca was nearby and followed his progress on the radio, but he could not face visiting him and, despite what is implied in Section 3, he refused to see his body.

'Ignacio's death is like mine, the trial run for mine,' he is thought to have told a friend. He began work on the elegy almost at once and it was published the following year.

Although Lorca had shown great sympathy for animals in the New York poem 'Office and Denunciation' he believed that the bullfight was an art form, showing the superiority 'of intelligence over instinct', so to him Ignacio was a hero. As in 'Guernica', the bull represents darkness and pain. The bulls of Guisando, referred to in Section 2, are ancient statues from Roman times.

1. La cogida y la muerte

A las cinco de la tarde.
Eran las cinco en punto de la tarde.
Un niño trajo la blanca sábana
a las cinco de la tarde.
Una espuerta de cal ya prevenida
a las cinco de la tarde.
Lo demás era muerte y solo muerte
a las cinco de la tarde.

El viento se llevó los algodones
a las cinco de la tarde.
Y el óxido sembró cristal y níquel
a las cinco de la tarde.
Ya luchan la paloma y el leopardo
a las cinco de la tarde.
Y un muslo con un asta desolada
a las cinco de la tarde.
Comenzaron los sones de bordón
a las cinco de la tarde.
Las campanas de arsénico y el humo
a las cinco de la tarde.
En las esquinas grupos de silencio
a las cinco de la tarde.
¡Y el toro solo corazón arriba!
a las cinco de la tarde.

Cuando el sudor de nieve fue llegando
a las cinco de la tarde
cuando la plaza se cubrió de yodo
a las cinco de la tarde,
la muerte puso huevos en la herida
a las cinco de la tarde.
A las cinco de la tarde.
A las cinco en punto de la tarde.

Un ataúd con ruedas es la cama
a las cinco de la tarde.
Huesos y flautas suenan en su oído
a las cinco de la tarde.

1. The Tossing and the Death

At five in the afternoon.
Exactly five in the afternoon.
A boy fetched the white sheet
at five in the afternoon.
A basket of lime made ready
at five in the afternoon.
The rest was death and death alone
at five in the afternoon.

The wind removed the cotton
at five in the afternoon.
The rust sowed glass and nickel
at five in the afternoon.
Now fight the leopard and the dove
at five in the afternoon.
A thigh with a forsaken horn
at five in the afternoon.
The sounds of the bourdon started
at five in the afternoon.
The bells of arsenic and smoke
at five in the afternoon.
Silent groups on corners
at five in the afternoon.
The bull alone was glad of heart
at five in the afternoon.

When sweat of snow was falling
at five in the afternoon,
when the ring was covered with iodine
at five in the afternoon,
then death laid eggs within the wound
at five in the afternoon.
At five in the afternoon
exactly five in the afternoon.

The bed is a wheeled coffin
at five in the afternoon.
Bones and flutes ring in his ears
at five in the afternoon.

El toro ya mugía por su frente
a las cinco de la tarde.
El cuarto se irisaba de agonía
a las cinco de la tarde.
A lo lejos ya viene la gangrena
a las cinco de la tarde.
Trompa de lirio por las verdes ingles
a las cinco de la tarde.
Las heridas quemaban como soles
a las cinco de la tarde,
y el gentío rompía las ventanas
a las cinco de la tarde.
A las cinco de la tarde.
¡Ay qué terribles cinco de la tarde!
¡Eran las cinco en todos los relojes!
¡Eran las cinco en sombra de la tarde!

2. La sangre derramada

¡Que no quiero verla!

Dile a la luna que venga,
que no quiero ver la sangre
de Ignacio sobre la arena.

¡Que no quiero verla!

La luna de par en par.
Caballo de nubes quietas,
y la plaza gris del sueño
con sauces en las barreras.

¡Que no quiero verla!
Que mi recuerdo se quema.
¡Avisad a los jazmines
con su blancura pequeña!

¡Que no quiero verla!

The bull roared through his forehead now
at five in the afternoon.
The room was luminous with pain
at five in the afternoon.
Far off, the gangrene coming
at five in the afternoon.
An iris horn through his green groins
at five in the afternoon.
Like suns the wounds were burning
at five in the afternoon,
the crowd was breaking windows
at five in the afternoon.
At five in the afternoon.
Ah, terrible five in the afternoon!
It was five by all the clocks!
The shadow of five in the afternoon.

2. The Spilled Blood

I do not want to see it!

Tell the moon to come,
I do not want to see
Ignacio's blood on the sand.

I do not want to see it!

The moon is open wide.
Horse of quiet clouds,
grey bull-ring of a dream
with willows on the barriers.

I do not want to see it!
Because my memory burns.
Give warning to the jasmines
with their little whiteness.

I do not want to see it!

La vaca del viejo mundo
pasaba su triste lengua
sobre un hocico de sangres
derramadas en la arena,
y los toros de Guisando,
casi muerte y casi piedra,
mugieron como dos siglos
hartos de pisar la tierra.
No.
¡Que no quiero verla!

Por las gradas sube Ignacio
con toda su muerte a cuestas.
Buscaba el amanecer,
y el amanecer no era.
Busca su perfil seguro,
y el sueño lo desorienta.
Buscaba su hermoso cuerpo
y encontró su sangre abierta.
¡No me digáis que la vea!
No quiero sentir el chorro
cada vez con menos fuerza;
ese chorro que ilumina
los tendidos y se vuelca
sobre la pana y el cuero
de muchedumbre sedienta.
¡Quién me grita que me asome!
No me digáis que la vea!

No se cerraron sus ojos
cuando vio los cuernos cerca,
pero las madres terribles
levantaron la cabeza.
Y a través de las ganaderías,
hubo un aire de voces secretas
que gritaban a toros celestes
mayorales de pálida niebla.
No hubo príncipe en Sevilla
que comparársele pueda,
ni espada como su espada,
ni corazón tan de veras.

The cow of the ancient world
passed her sorrowful tongue
over a snout of blood
spilled out upon the sand.
The bulls of Guisando,
almost death, almost stone,
roared like two centuries
weary with treading earth.
No.
I do not want to see it!

Ignacio mounts the steps
with all his death on his back.
He looked for the dawn
and the dawn was not there.
He seeks his confident profile,
the dream disorients it.
He sought his beautiful body
and found his opened blood.
Don't say that I should see it!
I don't want to feel the jet
grow weaker all the time;
that jet of blood which lights
the terraces, which spills
on corduroy and leather
of a thirsty crowd.
Who calls me to appear!
Don't say that I should see it!

He did not close his eyes
seeing the horns come near
but they lifted their heads,
the terrible mothers.
Across the ranches rose
a breath of secret voices
that foremen of pale mist
called to celestial bulls.
There was no prince in Sevilla
could be compared to him,
no sword like his sword
and no heart of such truth.

Como un río de leones
su maravillosa fuerza,
y como un torso de mármol
su dibujada prudencia.
Aire de Roma andaluza
le doraba la cabeza
donde su risa era un nardo
de sal y de inteligencia.
¡Que gran torero en la plaza!
¡Qué buen serrano en la sierra!
¡Qué blando con las espigas!
¡Qué duro con las espuelas!
¡Qué tierno con el rocío!
¡Qué deslumbrante en la feria!
¡Qué tremendo con las últimas
banderillas de tiniebla!

    Pero ya duerme sin fin.
Ya los musgos y la hierba
abren con dedos seguros
la flor de su calavera.
Y su sangre ya viene cantando:
cantando por marismas y praderas,
resbalando por cuernos ateridos,
vacilando su alma por la niebla,
tropezando con miles de pezuñas
como una larga, oscura, triste lengua,
para formar un charco de agonía
junto al Guadalquivir de las estrellas.
¡Oh blanco muro de España!
¡Oh negro toro de pena!
¡Oh sangre dura de Ignacio!
¡Oh ruiseñor de sus venas!
No.
¡Que no quiero verla!
Que no hay cáliz que la contenga,
que no hay golondrinas que se la beban,
no hay escarcha de luz que la enfríe,
no hay canto ni diluvio de azucenas,
no hay cristal que la cubra de plata.
No.
¡¡Yo no quiero verla!!

Like a river of lions
his marvellous strength,
and like a marble torso
his outstanding wisdom.
An air of Andalucían Rome
made his head appear golden,
and his laugh was a spikenard
of wit and intelligence.
How great a fighter of bulls!
How good a mountaineer!
How gentle with the corn
and how hard with the spurs!
How tender with the dew!
How dazzling in the fair!
How tremendous with the last
banderillas of darkness!

But now he sleeps without end.
Now the moss and the grass
with sure fingers unclose
the flower of his skull.
And now his blood comes singing
through marshes and through meadows,
sliding down stiffened horns,
wandering soulless through fog,
stumbling on thousands of hooves
like a long, dark, sad tongue
to form a pool of agony
by starry Guadalquivir.
Oh white wall of Spain!
Oh black bull of sorrow!
Oh hard blood of Ignacio!
Oh nightingale of his veins!
No.
I do not want to see it!
There is no cup to hold it,
no swallows that can drink it,
no frost of light to chill it,
no song nor flood of lilies,
no glass to make it silver.
No.
I do not want to see it!!

3. Cuerpo presente

La piedra es una frente donde los sueños gimen
sin tener agua curva ni cipreses helados.
La piedra es una espalda para llevar al tiempo
con árboles de lágrimas y cintas y planetas.

Yo he visto lluvias grises correr hacia las olas
levantando sus tiernos brazos acribillados,
para no ser cazadas por la piedra tendida
que desata sus miembros sin empapar la sangre.

Porque la piedra coge simientes y nublados,
esqueletos de alondras y lobos de penumbra;
pero no da sonidos, ni cristales, ni fuego,
sino plazas y plazas y otras plazas sin muros.

Ya está sobre la piedra Ignacio el bien nacido.
Ya se acabó; ¿qué pasa? Contemplad su figura:
la muerte le ha cubierto de pálidos azufres
y le ha puesto cabeza de oscuro minotauro.

Ya se acabó. La lluvia penetra por su boca.
El aire como loco deja su pecho hundido,
y el Amor, empapado con lágrimas de nieve,
se calienta en la cumbre de las ganaderías.

¿Qué dicen? Un silencio con hedores reposa.
Estamos con un cuerpo presente que se esfuma,
con una forma clara que tuvo ruiseñores
y la vemos llenarse de agujeros sin fondo.

¿Quién arruga el sudario? ¡No es verdad lo que dice!
Aquí no canta nadie, ni llora en el rincón,
ni pica las espuelas, ni espanta la serpiente:
aquí no quiero más que los ojos redondos
para ver ese cuerpo sin posible descanso.

Yo quiero ver aquí los hombres de voz dura.
Los que doman caballos y dominan los ríos:
los hombres que les suena el esqueleto y cantan
con una boca llena de sol y pedernales.

3. The Body Laid Out

The stone is a forehead on which dreams are moaning,
no winding water, no frozen evergreens.
The stone is a shoulder to carry time
with trees of tears, and ribbons, and planets.

I have seen grey rain flow towards the waves,
lifting its tender riddled arms,
not to be caught by the outstretched stone
which loosens limbs, and doesn't soak up the blood.

For the stone gathers seeds and dark clouds,
larks' skeletons, and wolves of shadow;
but it gives no sound, neither crystals nor fire,
only bull-rings, bull-rings, bull-rings without walls.

Now the well-born Ignacio lies on the stone.
It is finished; what is happening? Look at him:
death has covered him with pale sulphurs,
and placed on him a dark minotaur's head.

It is finished. Rain penetrates his mouth.
Air leaves his collapsed chest like a mad thing,
and Love, sodden with tears of snow,
warms itself above the herds of cattle.

What are they saying? A bad-smelling silence.
We are with a laid-out body that is fading,
with a noble form once rich in nightingales,
and we see it filled with bottomless holes.

Who is wrinkling the shroud? What he says is not true!
No one may sing here, or weep in a corner,
or prick his spurs, or frighten the snake:
here I want only wide-open eyes
to see that body; rest is impossible.

Here I want to see men with strong voices,
who tame horses and change the course of rivers:
men whose skeletons rattle and who sing
with a mouth full of sun and flints.

Aquí quiero yo verlos. Delante de la piedra.
Delante de este cuerpo con las riendas quebradas.
Yo quiero que me enseñen dónde está la salida
para este capitán atado por la muerte.

Yo quiero que me enseñen un llanto como un río
que tenga dulces nieblas y profundas orillas,
para llevar el cuerpo de Ignacio y que se pierda
sin escuchar el doble resuello de los toros.

Que se pierda en la plaza redonda de la luna
que finge cuando niña doliente res inmóvil;
que se pierda en la noche sin canto de los peces
y en la maleza blanca del humo congelado.

No quiero que le tapen la cara con pañuelos
para que se acostumbre con la muerte que lleva.
Vete, Ignacio: No sientas el caliente bramido.
Duerme, vuela, reposa: ¡También se muere el mar!

4. Alma ausente

No te conoce el toro ni la higuera,
ni caballos ni hormigas de tu casa.
No te conoce el niño ni la tarde
porque te has muerto para siempre.

No te conoce el lomo de la piedra,
ni el raso negro donde te destrozas.
No te conoce tu recuerdo mudo
porque te has muerto para siempre.

El otoño vendrá con caracolas,
uva de niebla y montes agrupados,
pero nadie querrá mirar tus ojos
porque te has muerto para siempre.

Here I want to see them. In front of the stone.
In front of this broken-reined body.
I want them to teach me where there is a way out
for this captain bound by death.

I want them to teach me a lament like a river
which has sweet mists and deep banks,
to bear Ignacio's body, and let him disappear
without hearing the bulls' double panting.

Let him disappear in the round bull-ring of the moon
which feigns when young a sad, unmoving beast;
let him disappear by night without the singing of fish
and in the frozen smoke's white thicket.

I do not want his face to be covered with handkerchieves,
I want him to grow used to his death.
Go, Ignacio. Do not feel the hot roaring.
Sleep, soar, rest! The sea dies too!

4. Absent Soul

The bull does not know you, nor the fig tree,
nor the horses nor the ants of your house.
The child does not know you, nor does the afternoon,
because you have died for ever.

The back of the stone slab does not know you,
nor the black satin shroud in which you crumble.
Your silent remembrance does not know you
because you have died for ever.

The autumn will come, shepherds blowing conch-shells,
misty grapes, and clusters of hills,
but no one will want to look into your eyes
because you have died for ever.

Porque te has muerto para siempre,
como todos los muertos de la Tierra,
como todos los muertos que se olvidan
en un montón de perros apagados.

No te conoce nadie. No. Pero yo te canto.
Yo canto para luego tu perfil y tu gracia.
La madurez insigne de tu conocimiento.
Tu apetencia de muerte y el gusto de su boca.
La tristeza que tuvo tu valiente alegría.

Tardará mucho tiempo en nacer, si es que nace,
un andaluz tan claro, tan rico de aventura.
Yo canto su elegancia con palabras que gimen
y recuerdo una brisa triste por los olivos.

Because you have died for ever,
like all of the dead of this earth,
like all the dead who are forgotten
in a heap of uncared-for dogs.

Nobody knows you. No. But I sing of you.
I sing of your grace for posterity.
Your profile, your maturity of thought.
Your love for death and the taste of his mouth.
The sadness in your light-hearted courage.

Not for a long time will be born, if at all,
an Andalucían so noble.
I sing of his elegance in words that moan,
and remember a sad breeze among the olives.

SONNETS OF DARK LOVE

SONETOS DEL AMOR OSCURO

1935-1936

SONNETS OF DARK LOVE

The eleven *Sonetos del amor oscuro*, as they are generally known, belong to the last year of Lorca's life. His brother believed he had written them

> for the purpose of acquiring discipline after the free forms of his last book of poems. These sonnets are today lost. The original manuscript was in the hands of a friend who died fighting during the Civil War.

He read them to various other poets, including Pablo Neruda and Vicente Aleixandre, who described them from memory as

> a prodigy of passion, of enthusiasm, of happiness, of torment, pure and ardent monument to love in which the prime material is now the poet's flesh, his heart, his soul wide open to his destruction. Wonderstruck, I gazed at him and said: 'Federico, what a heart! How much you must have loved, how much you must have suffered!'

He was in no great hurry to see them in print, and for almost half a century they were thought to have disappeared in the war years.

But, after all, the sonnets did survive. They were published in Spain in 1983 and are not yet widely known in this country. It should be said that the text may be corrupt and that, because of their tight structure, they are fiendishly difficult to translate.

They are not all equally good. For instance, the first eight lines of 'The loved one sleeps on the poet's breast' seem to me unremarkable; the last six, though, take one's breath away. The imagery – horses with green manes and violins streaming blood – is surrealist, but it also makes the sober point that the poet feels harassed because people are watching him with his friend and speculating about their relationship.

As usual, Lorca is intensely aware of death (which was even closer than he thought), and the love affair does not seem to have been a happy one. The sonnet about the 'enchanted city' of Cuenca, although it has the usual references to 'dolor' and 'pena', stands out because of its light-heartedness.

Soneto de la guirnalda de rosas

¡Esa guirnalda! ¡pronto! ¡que me muero!
¡Teje deprisa! ¡canta! ¡gime! ¡canta!
que la sombra me enturbia la garganta
y otra vez viene y mil la luz de enero.

Entre lo que me quieres y te quiero,
aire de estrellas y temblor de planta,
espesura de anémonas levanta
con oscuro gemir un año entero.

Goza el fresco paisaje de mi herida,
quiebra juncos y arroyos delicados.
Bebe en muslo de miel sangre vertida.

Pero ¡pronto! Que unidos, enlazados,
boca rota de amor y alma mordida,
el tiempo nos encuentre destrozados.

Soneto de la dulce queja

Tengo miedo a perder la maravilla
de tus ojos de estatua, y el acento
que de noche me pone en la mejilla
la solitaria rosa de tu aliento.

Tengo pena de ser en esta orilla
tronco sin ramas; y lo que más siento
es no tener la flor, pulpa o arcilla,
para el gusano de mi sufrimiento.

Si tú eres el tesoro oculto mío,
si eres mi cruz y mi dolor mojado,
si soy el perro de tu señorío,

no me dejes perder lo que he ganado
y decora las aguas de tu río
con hojas de mi otoño enajenado.

Sonnet of the Garland of Roses

That garland! hurry! how I long for it!
Weave it swiftly! sing! groan! sing!
How the shadow clouds my throat with pain,
a thousand times comes the January light.

Between what I want and what you desire,
a draught of stars, and plants trembling,
a thicket of anemones rising
with the dark groan of an entire year.

Enjoy the luscious landscape of my wound,
trample on reeds and dainty streams.
Drink in the thigh of honey my spilled blood.

But hurry! That united, intertwined,
with broken mouth of love and bitten souls,
time meets us, and we are destroyed.

Sonnet of the Sweet Complaint

I am afraid to lose the miracle
of your eyes – like a statue's – and the voice
which strokes my cheek, a thing nocturnal,
your breathing's solitary rose.

I have the pain of being on this shore,
trunk without branches. What I most regret
is having neither pulp, nor clay, nor flower
to feed the earthworm of my hurt.

If you are my hidden treasure,
if you're my cross, my tear-soaked grief,
if I am your lordship's dog,

don't let me lose what I have gained
and decorate the waters of your river
with my abandoned autumn's leaf.

Llagas de amor

Esta luz, este fuego que devora.
Este paisaje gris que me rodea.
Este dolor por una sola idea.
Esta angustia de cielo, mundo y hora.

   Este llanto de sangre que decora
lira sin pulso ya, lúbrica tea.
Este peso del mar que me golpea.
Este alacrán que por mi pecho mora.

   Son guirnalda de amor, cama de herido,
donde sin sueño, sueño tu presencia
entre las ruinas de mi pecho hundido.

   Y aunque busco la cumbre de prudencia
me da tu corazón valle tendido
con cicuta y pasión de amarga ciencia.

Soneto de la carta

Amor de mis entrañas, viva muerte,
en vano espero tu palabra escrita
y pienso, con la flor que se marchita,
que si vivo sin mí quiero perderte.

   El aire es inmortal, la piedra inerte
ni conoce la sombra ni la evita.
Corazón interior no necesita
la miel helada que la luna vierte.

   Pero yo te sufrí. Rasgué mis venas,
tigre y paloma, sobre tu cintura
en duelo de mordiscos y azucenas.

   Llena, pues, de palabras mi locura
o déjame vivir en mi serena
noche del alma para siempre oscura.

The Wounds of Love

This light, this fire that devours.
This grey landscape that surrounds me.
This obsession that torments me.
Anguish of heaven, world and hours.

This sobbing of the blood, draped round
a broken lyre, a slippery brand.
This sea which pounds me with its weight.
This scorpion dwelling in my heart.

Are all love's garland, and a bed,
where, without sleep, I try to rally,
and dream, amid the ruins, of your presence.

And though I seek the height of prudence
give me your heart, a spread-out valley
of hemlock and desire for bitter fruit.

Sonnet of the Letter

My inward love, my living death,
in vain I hope to see your written words,
and I think, with the flower that fades,
I'll lose you, if I live without myself.

Air is immortal, stone inert,
not knowing, nor avoiding shade.
The innermost heart has no need
of frozen honey which the moon pours out.

But I endured, I strummed my veins,
tiger and dove, across your waist,
duel of madonna lilies and of bites.

Fill, then, with words my lunacy,
oh, let me live in my serenity,
night of the soul, dark endlessly.

H

El poeta dice la verdad

Quiero llorar mi pena y te lo digo
para que tú me quieras y me llores
en un anochecer de ruiseñores
con un puñal, con besos y contigo.

Quiero matar al único testigo
para el asesinato de mis flores
y convertir mi llanto y mis sudores
en eterno montón de duro trigo.

Que no se acabe nunca la madeja
del te quiero me quieres, siempre ardida
con decrépito sol y luna vieja.

Que lo que no me des y no te pida
será para la muerte, que no deja
ni sombra por la carne estremecida.

El poeta habla por teléfono con el amor

Tu voz regó la duna de mi pecho
en la dulce cabina de madera.
Por el sur de mis pies fue primavera
y al norte de mi frente flor de helecho.

Pino de luz por el espacio estrecho
cantó sin alborada y sementera
y mi llanto prendió por vez primera
coronas de esperanza por el techo.

Dulce y lejana voz por mí vertida.
Dulce y lejana voz por mí gustada.
Lejana y dulce voz amortecida.

Lejana como oscura corza herida.
Dulce como un sollozo en la nevada.
¡Lejana y dulce en tuétano metida!

The Poet Speaks the Truth

I want to mourn my grief, I tell it to you
that you may want me and may weep for me
in a darkness of nightingales, where I see
a dagger, kisses and above all you.

I want to kill the only witness
to the assassination of my flowers
and to transform my grief and sweat
to an eternal mountain of hard wheat.

That we may never cease to weave the skein
of 'I want you', 'you want me', burning always
with a decrepit sun and an old moon;

That what I do not ask, and you don't give
to me, is death, which doesn't leave
even a shadow for the trembling flesh.

The Poet speaks to the loved one by telephone

Your voice watered the sandhill of my heart
in that sweet wooden cabin.
Spring blossomed to the south of my feet,
to the north, a flower of bracken.

A pine of light through the narrow space
sang without dawn, without a source,
while for the first time my grief
hung crowns of hope across the roof.

That sweet and distant voice poured through me.
That sweet and distant voice renewed me.
Sweet, distant, muffled tone.

Remote as a dark wounded doe.
And sweet as sobbing in the snow.
Sweet, distant, in my bone!

El poeta pregunta a su amor por la «Ciudad Encantada» de Cuenca

¿Te gustó la ciudad que gota a gota
labró el agua en el centro de los pinos?
¿Viste sueños y rostros y caminos
y muros de dolor que el aire azota?

¿Viste la grieta azul de luna rota
que el Júcar moja de cristal y trinos?
¿Han besado tus dedos los espinos
que coronan de amor piedra remota?

¿Te acordaste de mí cuando subías
al silencio que sufre la serpiente,
prisionera de grillos y de umbrías?

¿No viste por el aire transparente
una dalia de penas y alegrías
que te mandó mi corazón caliente?

Soneto gongorino en que el poeta manda a su amor una paloma

Este pichón del Turia que te mando,
de dulces ojos y de blanca pluma,
sobre laurel de Grecia vierte y suma
llama lenta de amor do estoy parando.

Su cándida virtud, su cuello blando,
en limo doble de caliente espuma,
con un temblor de escarcha, perla y bruma
la ausencia de tu boca está marcando.

Pasa la mano sobre su blancura
y verás qué nevada melodía
esparce en copos sobre tu hermosura.

Así mi corazón de noche y día,
preso en la cárcel del amor oscura,
llora sin verte su melancolía.

The Poet questions his lover on the 'enchanted city' of Cuenca

Did you like the city that water built
drop by drop in the heart of the pine woods?
Did you see visions, faces, roads,
and walls of pain for air to beat?

Did you see the blue chink of the broken moon
that Jucar wets with crystal and sweet sounds?
And did the hawthorns kiss your hands
that crown with love the distant stone?

Do you recall me when you mount
the silence which the snake endures,
a prisoner of crickets and of shades?

Didn't you see through the transparent air
a dahlia of gladness and despair
sent to you from my burning heart?

Gongorine sonnet in which the poet sends his loved one a pigeon

I send to you this Turian dove,
with sweet eyes and white plumage,
which spills, above the Grecian laurels,
a slow flame of love.

Its purity, its tender neck,
in double linen of warm froth,
trembling of frost, and pearl, and mist,
denotes the absence of your lips.

Pass your hand across this dove
and you will see its snowy melody
scatter in flakes above your beauty.

Thus my heart by night and day,
sealed in the prison of dark love,
weeps and grieves while you're away.

[¡Ay voz secreta del amor oscuro!]

¡Ay voz secreta del amor oscuro!
¡ay balido sin lanas! ¡ay herida!
¡ay aguja de hiel, camelia hundida!
¡ay corriente sin mar, ciudad sin muro!

¡Ay noche inmensa de perfil seguro,
montaña celestial de angustia erguida!
¡Ay perro en corazón, voz perseguida!
silencio sin confín, lirio maduro!

Huye de mí, caliente voz de hielo,
no me quieras perder en la maleza
donde sin fruto gimen carne y cielo.

Deja el duro marfil de mi cabeza,
apiádate de mí, ¡rompe mi duelo!,
¡que soy amor, que soy naturaleza!

El amor duerme en el pecho del poeta

Tú nunca entenderás lo que te quiero
porque duermes en mí y estás dormido.
Yo te oculto llorando, perseguido
por una voz de penetrante acero.

Norma que agita igual carne y lucero
traspasa ya mi pecho dolorido
y las turbias palabras han mordido
las alas de tu espíritu severo.

Grupo de gente salta en los jardines
esperando tu cuerpo y mi agonía
en caballos de luz y verdes crines.

Pero sigue durmiendo, vida mía.
¡Oye mi sangre rota en los violines!
¡Mira que nos acechan todavía!

'Ah, secret voice of dark love'

Ah, secret voice of dark love,
wound, bleating without wool!
withered camelia, bitter needle!
current without sea, city with no wall!

Tremendous night with sharp-edged profile,
celestial mountain, narrow defile!
dog in the heart, receding voice!
unending silence, full-blown iris!

Leave me alone, hot voice of ice,
and do not ask me to get lost
where fruitless, in the weeds, groan heaven and flesh.

Leave the hard ivory of my skull for ever,
have pity on me, stop the torture!
I am love and I am nature!

The loved one sleeps on the poet's breast

You're never going to realise what I feel
because you sleep on me and you are sleeping.
And that's why I conceal you, weeping,
chased by a voice of penetrating steel.

The rule which shakes both star and fleshly things
pierces my sore breast now
and the cloudy words have bitten through
your unkind spirit's wings.

A group of people leap into the gardens
awaiting your body and my pain
upon horses of light, with manes of green.

But follow me, my love, unconscious.
Listen to my smashed blood in the violins!
And see how they're still spying on us!

Noche del amor insomne

Noche arriba los dos con luna llena,
yo me puse a llorar y tú reías.
Tu desdén era un dios, las quejas mías
momentos y palomas en cadena.

  Noche abajo los dos. Cristal de pena,
llorabas tú por hondas lejanías.
Mi dolor era un grupo de agonías
sobre tu débil corazón de arena.

  La aurora nos unió sobre la cama,
las bocas puestas sobre el chorro helado
de una sangre sin fin que se derrama.

  Y el sol entró por el balcón cerrado
y el coral de la vida abrió su rama
sobre mi corazón amortajado.

Night of Sleepless Love

Night above the two, with a full moon.
I began to weep, you laughed.
Your contempt was like a god,
my tears were doves and moments in a chain.

Night beneath the two. Crystal of grief,
you sobbed through deep distances.
My pain was a cluster of agonies
on your frail heart of sand.

Dawn brought us together on the bed,
mouths placed upon a freezing jet
of blood that flows without an end.

The sun came through a window, which was closed.
Life's coral spread
its branch, above my shrouded heart.

THEORY AND FUNCTION
OF THE *DUENDE*
JUEGA Y TEORÍA DEL DUENDE
1933

THEORY AND FUNCTION OF THE *DUENDE*

The following is the text of a lecture which Lorca gave in Havana and Buenos Aires, and which gives us some clue to understanding his poetry. However, it is so idiosyncratic, and so full of allusions to the culture he grew up in, that many readers may be baffled.

'*Duende*' means literally imp, goblin, demon. But what he is really talking about is the quality which distinguishes great art, in any medium, from that which is merely competent, 'a mysterious power which everyone feels and which no philosopher can explain'. It is this quality which makes us passionately admire one particular poem, piece of music or picture after we have heard or seen thousands which are good in themselves. We may be able to give reasons for our choice, but, ultimately, it is a mystery.

For Lorca, this power is intimately connected with the 'hidden spirit of suffering Spain'. He finds the *duende* in flamenco, the bullfight, and the ancient ballads he quotes which, like his own poetry, are about love and death. 'All that has dark sounds has *duende*,' he proclaims. It has nothing to do with intellect, it is in the blood, and it exists only where there is a possibility of death. We do not need to know all the works of art to which Lorca refers to understand that he is telling us something about the 'demon' which drove him.

On page 222 he makes a mistake in his reference to Luther at Nüremberg. I could have corrected this to Wartberg in my translation.

Juega y teoría del duende

Ladies and Gentlemen:

From the year 1918, when I entered the Students' Residence in Madrid, until 1928, when I left it, completing my studies in philosophy and literature, I heard in that distinguished place, where the old Spanish aristocracy came to counteract the frivolity of French seaside resorts, more than a thousand conferences.

Longing for air and sun, I grew very bored, and when I left I felt covered with a thin layer of ash almost to the point of my becoming a pepper-pot of irritation.

No. I didn't want to bring into this room the terrible blowfly of boredom which strings together all heads with a thin thread of dreams and which puts in an audience's eyes little bundles of pins.

To speak plainly, in that range of my poetic voice which does not possess wooden lights, or hemlock loops, or sheep which change to blades of irony, I'm going to see if I can give a simple lecture on the hidden spirit of suffering Spain.

Anyone who goes to that stretched-out bullskin between the Júcar, Guadalete, Sil or Pisuerga (I don't want to name the waters, coloured like a lion's mane, which shake the Plata) will fairly often hear the words, 'This has much *duende*.' Manuel Torres, a great Andalucían artist, said to someone who was singing: 'You have a voice, you know the style, but you will never be a great success, because you have no *duende*.'

All over Andalucía, from the rock of Jaén to the shell of Cádiz, people speak constantly of the duende and recognise it with a sure instinct when it appears.

The marvellous singer *El Lebrijano*, creator of the *Debla*, said: 'No one is as good as me on the days when I sing with *duende*.' The old gypsy dancer *La Malena* once exclaimed, on hearing Brailowsky play a piece of Bach: 'Olé! That's got *duende*!', and she was bored with Gluck and with Brahms and with Darius Milhaud. And Manuel Torres, a man with more culture in his blood than anyone I have known, on listening to Falla playing his own *Nocturno del Generalife* coined this splendid phrase: 'All that has dark sounds has *duende*.' And there is no greater truth.

These dark sounds are the mystery, the roots pushing into the soil which we all know, which we all ignore, but from which comes what is real in art. Dark sounds, said the popular artist of Spain, and he agrees with Goethe, who defined the *duende* when he spoke of Paganini: 'A mysterious power which everyone feels and which no philosopher can explain.'

So, then, the *duende* is a power and not a form of behaviour, a struggle, not a mode of thought. I have heard an old master-guitarist say: 'The *duende* isn't in your throat, the *duende* wells up from inside the soles of your feet.' That means it is not a question of ability, but of true living style, of blood, of ancient culture, of the act of creation.

This 'mysterious power which everyone feels and which no philosopher can explain' is, in short, the spirit of the earth, the same *duende* which seized the heart of Nietzsche, who had been seeking it in its external forms on the Rialto bridge or in the music of Bizet, without finding it and without knowing that the *duende* he sought had jumped from the mysterious Greeks to the dancers of Cádiz or the mangled Dionysiac cry of Silverio's *siguiriya*.

So I don't want anyone to confuse the *duende* with the theological demon of doubt, at which Luther in a Bacchic mood threw an inkpot in Nüremberg, nor with the Catholic devil, destructive and unintelligent, who disguises himself as a female dog to get into convents.

No. The *duende* that I speak of, dark and quivering, is a descendant of Socrates' happy demon, marble and salt, who indignantly scratched him the day he took hemlock, and of the other melancholy demon of Descartes, small as a green almond, who got tired of lines and circles and went down by the canals to hear drunken sailors sing.

Every man – Nietzsche would say, every artist – climbs each stair in the tower of his own perfection at the cost of his struggle with a *duende* – not with an angel, as some say, or with a muse. We must make this fundamental distinction to get to the root of the work.

The angel guides and gives gifts like St Raphael, defends and saves like St Michael, forewarns like St Gabriel. The angel is radiant, but he flies over men's heads, above us, he pours out his grace while man effortlessly achieves his work, his sympathy or his dance. The angel of the road to Damascus and the one who came through the opening of the little balcony at Assisi, or the angel who followed the steps of Enrique Susón, *commands* us and we cannot resist his light, because he waves his steely wings in the ambit of those who are predestined.

The muse dictates and, sometimes, inspires. She can do relatively little, because she is now so distant and exhausted (I have seen her twice) that I had to put half a marble heart inside her. The poets of the muse hear voices and do not know their origin, but they are from the muse who inspires them and sometimes makes a meal of them. So it was with Apollinaire, a great poet destroyed by the horrible muse with whom he was painted by the divine, angelic Rousseau. The muse awakes the intellect, brings pillared landscapes and a false flavour of laurel. Intellect is often the enemy of poetry because it imitates too much, because it raises the poet to a sharp-edged throne and makes him forget he might soon be eaten by ants, or a great arsenic lobster might fall on his head. Against this the muses in monocles or in a small salon's cool lacquered rose are helpless.

Angel and muse come from outside; the angel gives light and the muse gives shape (Hesiod learned from them). Gold leaf or pleat of tunics, the poet receives norms in his laurel grove. The *duende*, though, must be awakened in the deepest dwellings of blood.

We must push away the angel and kick out the muse, and cease to fear the violet fragrance which is breathed from eighteenth-century poetry and from the great telescope with the sickly muse of limits asleep in its glass.

The real struggle is with the *duende*.

The ways to seek God are known, the rough way of the hermit or the mystic's subtle way. With a tower like St Teresa, or by three paths like St John of the Cross. And even though we must cry with Isaiah's voice, 'Truly you are the hidden God', in the end God sends his first thorns of fire to those who seek him.

But there is no map, no formula to seek the *duende*. We only know that it burns the blood like glass, that it drains you, that it rejects all the sweet geometry you have learned, that it breaks with style, that it makes Goya – the master of grey, silver and pink like the best English artists – paint horrible bitumen black with his knees and his fists. Or it strips Jacint Verdaguer in the cold Pyrenees, or takes Jorge Manrique to await death in Ocaña's wasteland, or clothes Rimbaud's delicate body in an acrobat's green suit, or puts the eyes of a dead fish on Count Lautréamont in the boulevard, at dawn.

The great artists of southern Spain, gypsy or flamenco, know as they sing, dance or play that no emotion is possible without the *duende*. They may deceive you by giving the impression of *duende* when it isn't there, as you are deceived every day by authors, painters or literary fashions without *duende*, but if you pay attention, and are not indifferent, you will discover the clumsy fraud and put it to flight.

Once, the Andalucían singer Pastora Pavón, *La Niña de los Peines*

['The Girl with the Combs'], a sombre Spanish genius with an imagination like that of Goya or Rafael 'the Cock', was singing in a tavern at Cádiz. She played with her voice of shadow and of melted tin, her voice covered with moss, and she tangled it in her hair or drenched it in *manzanilla* or lost it in dark, distant woods. But it was no good, useless. The audience remained unmoved.

Ignacio Espeleta was there, handsome as a Roman tortoise, who once, on being asked, 'Why don't you work?' replied, with a smile worthy of Argantonio, 'Why should I work, if I come from Cádiz?'

Eloísa was there too, the fiery aristocratic whore of Sevilla, a direct descendant of Soledad Vargas, who in 1930 declined to marry a Rothschild because he was not her equal in blood. The Floridas were there, who are believed to be butchers, but are really ancient priests who still sacrifice bulls to Geryon, and in a corner was the stately rancher Don Pablo Murube, looking like a Cretan mask. Pastora Pavón ended her song amid silence. Only a very small man, one of those little dancers who suddenly come out from the bottles of brandy, sarcastically said in a very low voice, '*Viva Paris!*', as if to say: 'Here we don't care about talent, or technique, or mastery. We care for something else'.

Then *La Niña de los Peines* jumped up like a madwoman, crippled like a medieval mourner, drank in one gulp a large glass of fiery *cazalla*, and sat down to sing without a voice, without breath, without subtlety, with a burning throat, but…with *duende*. To do it she needed to destroy all the scaffolding of the song to make way for a furious and blazing *duende*, friend of the desert winds, that made the listeners tear their clothes with almost the same rhythm as West Indians at their rites, crowded before St Barbara's statue.

La Niña de los Peines had to wrench her voice, because she knew that the fastidious listeners wanted not forms but the essence of form, pure music with hardly a body to hold itself up in the air. She had to weaken her own skills and safeguards, to get away from her muse and remain defenceless, so that her *duende* would come and deign to fight her hand-to-hand. And how she sang! She didn't play with her voice now, her voice was a jet of blood dignified by grief and sincerity, and it opened like a hand with ten fingers through the pierced but stormy feet of a Christ by Juan de Juni.

The coming of the *duende* always presupposes a deep change in all the old forms. It gives a sense of freshness, totally unknown before, with a quality of the newly created rose, of miracle. It succeeds in producing an almost religious fervour.

In all Arabic music, dance, song or elegy, the coming of the *duende* is greeted with energetic cries of '*Allah! Allah!*', '*God! God!*', very similar to the bullfighters' '*Olé!*' In all the songs of southern Spain the *duende*'s appearance is followed by sincere cries of '*Long live God!*' – a profound, human, tender cry of communication with God through the five senses, thanks to the *duende* which moves the voice and body of the dancer, a real and poetic flight from this world, as pure as that obtained by the rare seventeenth-century poet Pedro Soto de Rojas across seven gardens, or that of St John Climacus on his trembling ladder of grief.

Naturally, when this flight from the world is achieved, everyone feels its effects – the initiated, seeing how style can conquer mere matter, and the uneducated, with an indefinable but real emotion. Years ago, in a dancing contest at Jerez de la Frontera, an old woman of eighty carried off the prize against beautiful women and girls with waists like water, simply by raising her arms, lifting her head and beating her foot on the stage. But in that reunion of muses and angels, beauties of form and beauties of smile, that moribund *duende* which dragged its wings of rusty knives along the ground was bound to win, and did.

All the arts are capable of *duende*, but it finds most scope, naturally, in music, dance and spoken poetry. They need a living body to interpret them, since they are forms that are born and die endlessly and raise their contours in the exact present. The *duende* of the musician often passes to the *duende* of the interpreter, and at other times, when the musician or poet are not up to it, the interpreter's *duende* – and this is interesting – creates a new marvel which has little in common with the original work. Such is the case of Eleonora Duse, full of *duende*, who sought out unsuccessful works and made them triumph, thanks to what she put into them. Or Paganini, who according to Goethe could make profound music out of very ordinary stuff. Or a charming girl in Puerto de Santa María, whom I saw sing and dance the dreadful Italian song 'O Marí!' with such rhythm, pauses and meaning that she made of the Italian trash a hard snake of raised gold.

What was really happening was that they were discovering a new thing which had never been seen before, infusing living blood and skill in vessels empty of expression.

All arts, and all countries, can produce the *duende*, the angel and the muse. So Germany has, with exceptions, a muse, and Italy a permanent angel, but Spain is perpetually moved by the *duende*, for it is an ancient land of music and dance, where the *duende* squeezes lemons of dawn, and a land of death, a land open to death.

In every country death is an end. Death comes and the blinds are drawn. In Spain, no. In Spain they are lifted. Many people there live between walls until the day they die and are brought out into the sun. A dead man in Spain is more alive than a dead man anywhere else on earth: his profile has a cutting edge like a barber's razor. The joke about death and its silent contemplation are familiar to Spaniards. From Quevedo's *Dream of the Skulls* to the *Rotting Bishop* of Valdés Leal, and from the seventeenth-century Marbella, dead in childbirth on the road, who said:

La sangre de mis entrañas	The blood of my entrails
cubriendo el caballo está;	covers the horse;
las patas de tu caballo	the hooves of your horse
echan fuego de alquitrán	create sparks of tar

to the young man of Salamanca, recently killed by a bull, who cried:

Amigos, que yo me muero;	Friends, I am dying;
amigos, yo estoy muy malo.	friends, I'm very bad.
Tres pañuelos tengo dentro	Three handkerchieves I have inside
y este que meto son cuatro.	and this is the fourth.

…there is a barrier made of flowers of saltpetre, where there rises a people contemplating death, with Jeremiah's verses on their roughest side, and fragrant cypress on the side that is most lyrical. But it is a land where the most important thing of all has a final metallic value of death. The knife and the cartwheel, the razor and the pointed beards of herdsmen, the bald moon, the fly, damp larders, rubble, lace-enshrouded saints, lime, and the cutting outline of eaves and balconies possess, in Spain, little grasses of death, allusions and voices which the alert mind can pick up, which summon our memory with the rigid wind of our own passing. It is no accident that all Spanish art is bound to our soil, full of thistles and definitive stones. The lament of Pleberio or the dances of the great Josef María de Valdivielso are not isolated instances; it is no accident that this Spanish love song stands out from all the ballads of Europe:

Si tú eres mi linda amiga,	'If you are my sweetheart,
¿cómo no me miras, di?	why don't you look at me?'
Ojos con que te miraba	'The eyes with which I looked at you
a la sombra se los di.	I gave to the shadow.'
Si tú eres mi linda amiga,	'If you are my sweetheart,
¿cómo no me besas, di?	then why don't you kiss me?'
labios con que te besaba	'The lips with which I kissed you
a la tierra se los di.	I gave to the earth.'
Si tú eres mi linda amiga,	'If you are my sweetheart,
¿cómo no me abrazas, di?	why don't you embrace me?'
Brazos con que te abrazaba	'The arms I embraced you with
de gusanos los cubrí.	I covered with worms.'

Nor is it strange to find among our earliest lyrics, this song:

Dentro del vergel	In the garden
moriré.	I shall die.
Dentro del rosal	In the rose bush
matar me han.	they will kill me.
Yo me iba, mi madre,	I was going, mother,
las roses coger,	to pick some roses,
hallara la muerte	I met death
dentro del vergel.	in the garden.
Yo me iba, mi madre,	I was going, mother,
las rosas cortar,	to cut some roses,
hallara la muerte	I met death
dentro del rosal.	in the rose bush.
Dentro del vergel	In the garden
moriré,	I shall die,
dentro del rosal,	in the rose bush
matar me han.	they will kill me.

The painter Zurbarán's moon-frozen heads, El Greco's yellow of butter and of lightning, the prose of Father Sigüenza, Goya's entire work, the apse of the church in Escorial, all polychrome sculpture, the crypt of Osuna's ducal house, 'Death with the Guitar' in the Benaventes' chapel at Medina de Rioseco – all these are the cultural equivalent to the pilgrimages of San Andrés de Teixido, where the dead have a place in the procession, to the dead-songs sung by Asturian women with flaming lanterns on a November night, to the sibyl's song and dance in the cathedrals of Mallorca and Toledo, to the dark Tortosan '*In Recort*' and the innumerable rites of Good Friday, which, together with the highly civilised spectacle of bull-fighting, form the popular triumph of death in Spain. In the whole world, only Mexico can compare with my country.

When the muse sees death, she shuts the door or raises a plinth or displays an urn and writes, with her waxen hand, an epitaph, but next she tears her laurel wreath in a silence wavering between two breezes. Beneath the broken arch of the ode, she mournfully binds the exact flowers which the Italians painted in the fifteenth century, and calls Lucretius' trusted cockerel to put unexpected shadows to flight.

When the angel sees death, he flies in slow circles and weaves with tears of frost and narcissus the elegy we have seen trembling in Keats' hands, and those of Villasandino, Herrera, Bécquer and Juan Ramón Jiménez. But how horrified the angel will be if he feels a spider, even a little one, on his tender rosy foot!

But the *duende* doesn't come if it sees no possibility of death, if it doesn't know it will haunt the house of death, if it doesn't mean to shake those branches which we all carry and which neither are, nor will be, comforted.

In idea, sound or gesture the *duende* likes a straight fight with the creator on the rim of the well. Angel and muse escape with violin or compass; the *duende* wounds, and in healing this wound, which never closes, is the exceptional, the creative part of man's work.

The magical quality of a poem consists in being always full of *duende*, to baptise all those who admire it with dark water. Because with duende it is easier to love, to understand, and one is *certain* to be loved and underderstood, and this struggle for expression and communication in poetry becomes a mortal struggle at times.

Remember the case of St Teresa, possessed with flamenco and *duende*. Flamenco not because she stopped an angry bull with three magnificent passes, which she did; not because she showed off her good looks before the friar Juan de la Miseria and not because she slapped the Papal Nuncio, but for being one of the few creatures whose *duende* (not angel, for an angel attacks no one) transfixed her with a dart, wanting to kill her for discovering its last secret, the delicate bridge which joins the five senses to that centre of living flesh, living cloud, living sea, of timeless love.

This valiant conqueror of the *duende* was quite unlike Philip of Austria, who, longingly seeking the angel and muse of theology, found himself imprisoned by the *duende*'s cold ardours in that building El Escorial, whose geometry borders on dream and where the duende dons the muse's mask for the eternal punishment of the great king.

We have said that the *duende* likes the edge, the wound, and approaches places where the forms unite in a yearning greater than their visible expressions.

In Spain (as among Eastern peoples, where the dance is a religious expression), the *duende* has a boundless scope in the bodies of the dancers of Cádiz, praised by Martial, in the breasts of singers, praised by Juvenal, and in the whole liturgy of bullfighting, an authentic religious drama where, as in the mass, a god is worshipped and is sacrificed.

It seems as if all the *duende* in the ancient world has come together in this perfect ritual, exhibiting the culture and the great sensibility of a people who discover man's highest anger, spleen and grief. Nobody is amused by Spanish dance nor by the bullfight; the *duende* ensures we suffer through the drama, in living forms, and prepares the stairs for a flight from surrounding reality.

The *duende* operates on a dancer's body like wind on the sand.

With magic power, it changes a girl into a paralytic of the moon, or fills with adolescent blushes an old broken man who is begging round the wine shops for alms. It gives a head of hair the smell of a night-time harbour, and at each moment it moves the arms with gestures which have always been the mothers of dance.

But it is impossible to repeat oneself, better to emphasise it. The *duende* does not repeat itself, any more than the shapes of the sea in a storm.

In bullfighting it acquires its most impressive tones, because on the one side it has to fight with death, which might destroy it, and on the other with geometry, the fundamental base and measure of the ritual.

The bull has its orbit; the bullfighter his, and between the two orbits is a point of danger which is the vertex of the terrible game.

You can have the muse with the *muleta* and the angel with the *banderillas* and pretend to be a good bullfighter, but in the work with the cape, when the bull is still unwounded, and in the moment of killing, you need the help of the *duende* to thrust home the artistic truth.

The bullfighter who alarms the public by taking risks is not bullfighting, he is absurdly *playing with his life*, which any man can do. But the bullfighter bitten by the *duende* gives a lesson of Pythagorean music, and makes us forget that he is constantly throwing his heart at the horns.

Lagartijo with his Roman *duende*, Joselito with his Jewish *duende*, Belmonte with his baroque *duende* and Cagancho with his gypsy *duende*, from the twilight of the bull-ring they show poets, painters and musicians four great paths of the Spanish tradition.

Spain is the only country where death is a national spectacle, where death sounds great bugles on the arrival of spring. Its art is always governed by an artful *duende* which gives it its uniqueness and its quality of invention.

The *duende* that fills with blood, for the first time in sculpture, the cheeks of the saints of the great Mateo de Compostela, is the *duende* which makes St John of the Cross groan or which scalds naked nymphs in Lope de Vega's religious sonnets.

The *duende* which raised the tower of Sahagún or worked hot bricks in Calatayud or Teruel is the same which breaks El Greco's clouds, kicks Quevedo's bailiffs till they roll, and inspires Goya's weird dreams.

When it rains, it brings out a *duende*-haunted Velázquez, in secret, behind his monarchical greys; when it snows it brings out a naked

Herrera to prove that cold doesn't kill; when it burns, it puts Berruguete in the midst of flames and makes him invent a new space for sculpture.

The muse of Góngora and Garcilaso's angel must drop the laurel wreath when the *duende* of St John of the Cross goes by, when 'the wounded stag appears above the hill'.

Gonzalo de Berceo's muse and the angel of the archpriest of Hita must withdraw to let Jorge Manrique pass when he comes fatally wounded to the gates of Belmonte castle. The muse of Gregorio Hernández and the angel of José de Mora must give way to the *duende*, weeping tears of Mena's blood, and Martínez Montañés' *duende* with the head of an Assyrian bull. And the melancholy muse of Cataluña and the damp angel of Galicia have to look with loving wonder at Castilla's *duende*, so far from the warm bread and the sweet cow that grazes in the normality of sweeping sky and dry earth.

The *duende* of Quevedo and the *duende* of Cervantes, one with green phosphorus anemones, the other with plaster anemones of Ruidera, crown the altarpiece of the *duende* of Spain.

Each art has, as is natural, a *duende* of a distinct kind, but all their roots join at a point where the dark sounds of Manuel Torres well up. It is ultimate matter, the common base, uncontrollable and trembling, of wood, sound, fabric and words.

Dark sounds behind which, in tender intimacy, are volcanoes, ants, zephyrs and the great night that clasps her waist with the Milky Way.

Ladies and gentlemen: I have raised three arches and with a clumsy hand have placed in them the muse, the angel and the *duende*.

The muse remains quiet; she can have a tunic in small pleats or the cow's eyes that regard Pompeii or the big nose with four faces painted by Picasso, her great friend. The angel can shake Antonello de Messina's hair, Lippi's tunic and Massolino or Rousseau's violin.

The *duende*...Where is the *duende*? Through the empty arch enters a wind of the mind, which blows over the heads of the dead insistently, searching for new landscapes, accents we never knew. A wind with a smell of children's spittle, crushed grass and a jellyfish veil which announces the constant baptism of newly created things.

Index of English titles and first lines

(Titles are in italics, first lines in roman type)

Index of Spanish titles and first lines

AUTHORS PUBLISHED BY

BLOODAXE BOOKS

FLEUR ADCOCK
GÖSTA ÅGREN
ANNA AKHMATOVA
SIMON ARMITAGE
NEIL ASTLEY
ATTILA THE STOCKBROKER
ANNEMARIE AUSTIN
SHIRLEY BAKER
GEREME BARMÉ
MARTIN BELL
CONNIE BENSLEY
STEPHEN BERG
YVES BONNEFOY
MARTIN BOOTH
KAMAU BRATHWAITE
GORDON BROWN
BASIL BUNTING
CIARAN CARSON
ANGELA CARTER
JOHN CASSIDY
JAROSLAV CEJKA
MICHAL CERNÍK
AIMÉ CÉSAIRE
SID CHAPLIN
RENÉ CHAR
GEORGE CHARLTON
EILÉAN NÍ CHUILLEANÁIN
KILLARNEY CLARY
BRENDAN CLEARY
JACK CLEMO
HARRY CLIFTON
JACK COMMON
STEWART CONN
NOEL CONNOR
DAVID CONSTANTINE
CHARLOTTE CORY
JENI COUZYN
HART CRANE
ADAM CZERNIAWSKI
PETER DIDSBURY
STEPHEN DOBYNS
MAURA DOOLEY
KATIE DONOVAN
JOHN DREW
IAN DUHIG
HELEN DUNMORE
DOUGLAS DUNN
STEPHEN DUNSTAN
JACQUES DUPIN
G.F. DUTTON
LAURIS EDMOND
ALISTAIR ELLIOT
STEVE ELLIS
ODYSSEUS ELYTIS
EURIPIDES
DAVID FERRY

EVA FIGES
SYLVA FISCHEROVÁ
TONY FLYNN
VICTORIA FORDE
TUA FORSSTRÖM
JIMMY FORSYTH
LINDA FRANCE
ELIZABETH GARRETT
ARTHUR GIBSON
PAMELA GILLILAN
ANDREW GREIG
JOHN GREENING
PHILIP GROSS
JOSEF HANZLÍK
TONY HARRISON
ANNE HÉBERT
HAROLD HESLOP
DOROTHY HEWETT
FRIEDRICH HÖLDERLIN
MIROSLAV HOLUB
FRANCES HOROVITZ
DOUGLAS HOUSTON
JOHN HUGHES
PAUL HYLAND
KATHLEEN JAMIE
VLADIMÍR JANOVIC
B.S. JOHNSON
LINTON KWESI JOHNSON
JOOLZ
JENNY JOSEPH
SYLVIA KANTARIS
JACKIE KAY
BRENDAN KENNELLY
SIRKKA-LIISA KONTTINEN
JEAN HANFF KORELITZ
DENISE LEVERTOV
HERBERT LOMAS
MARION LOMAX
EDNA LONGLEY
FEDERICO GARCÍA LORCA
GEORGE MacBETH
PETER McDONALD
DAVID McDUFF
MEDBH McGUCKIAN
MAIRI MacINNES
CHRISTINE McNEILL
OSIP MANDELSTAM
GERALD MANGAN
E.A. MARKHAM
WILLIAM MARTIN
JILL MAUGHAN
GLYN MAXWELL
HENRI MICHAUX
JOHN MINFORD
ADRIAN MITCHELL
JOHN MONTAGUE

EUGENIO MONTALE
DAVID MORLEY
RICHARD MURPHY
BILL NAUGHTON
SEAN O'BRIEN
JULIE O'CALLAGHAN
JOHN OLDHAM
MICHEAL O'SIADHAIL
TOM PAULIN
GYÖRGY PETRI
TOM PICKARD
JILL PIRRIE
SIMON RAE
DEBORAH RANDALL
IRINA RATUSHINSKAYA
DIANE RAWSON
MARIA RAZUMOVSKY
JEREMY REED
PETER REDGROVE
ANNE ROUSE
CAROL RUMENS
LAWRENCE SAIL
EVA SALZMAN
SAPPHO
WILLIAM SCAMMELL
DAVID SCOTT
JO SHAPCOTT
SIR ROY SHAW
JAMES SIMMONS
MATT SIMPSON
LEMN SISSAY
DAVE SMITH
KEN SMITH
SEAN SMITH
STEPHEN SMITH
EDITH SÖDERGRAN
PIOTR SOMMER
MARIN SORESCU
LEOPOLD STAFF
PAULINE STAINER
EIRA STENBERG
MARTIN STOKES
KAREL SYS
RABINDRANATH TAGORE
JEAN TARDIEU
D.M. THOMAS
R.S. THOMAS
TOMAS TRANSTRÖMER
MARINA TSVETAYEVA
FRED VOSS
ALAN WEARNE
NIGEL WELLS
C.K. WILLIAMS
JOHN HARTLEY WILLIAMS
JAMES WRIGHT
BENJAMIN ZEPHANIAH

For a complete catalogue of books published by Bloodaxe, pleaee write to:

Bloodaxe Books Ltd, P.O. Box 1SN, Newcastle upon Tyne NE99 1SN.